# WHEN IT HAPPENED IN
# Scotland

# WHEN IT HAPPENED IN
# Scotland

A VERY QUICK HISTORY
Including
Kings and Queens,
Battles & Major Events
Compiled in Chronological Order,
for All Those Who
CANNOT REMEMBER
*or Never Learnt*
THE NATION'S STORY

George Chamier

With illustrations by Lachlan Campbell

CONSTABLE • LONDON

Constable & Robinson Ltd
3 The Lanchesters
162 Fulham Palace Road
London W6 9ER
www.constablerobinson.com

Published by Constable,
an imprint of Constable & Robinson, 2009



A copy of the British Library Cataloguing in Publication Data is available from the British Library

ISBN: 978-1-84901-006-1

Printed and bound in the EU

1 3 5 7 9 10 8 6 4 2

PEFC/16-33-111
CATG-PEFC-052
www.pefc.org

*In memory of my mother*
*and to the members, all over the world,*
*of the Clan Munro*

# PREFACE

Scotland's history is richly encrusted with myth and legend. In part this is because the Scots have always been a nation of storytellers. John Barbour's *The Brus* (1375), his long narrative poem in praise of King Robert the Bruce, opens thus:

> Storys to rede are delitabell,
> Suppos that thai be nocht bot fabill.*

And 'nocht bot fabill' is just what many received ideas about Scotland's history are. Clan sagas, ballads and stories of witchcraft and enchantment are so interwoven with the historical record that it is sometimes difficult to know where fact ends and the fiction begins. The celebrated ballad *Sir Patrick Spens* ('The King sits in Dunfermline town/ Drinking of the blood-red wine') is clearly connected with the story of the Maid of Norway (*see* 1286) but hardly gives a reliable account of what happened. Sir Walter Scott's Jacobite novels and the Highland Revival of the early 1800s were responsible for a tourist's picture of Scotland that is recognized around the world, but scarcely reflected the reality of its own time, let alone of Scotland today.

Many of the popular misconceptions of Scottish history are the result of Scots asserting their difference and independence from their bigger neighbour to the south.

* 'Stories to read are delightful, suppose that they are nothing but fable.'

Even the origin myth of Gaythelus (*see* 1249) was designed to prove that the pedigree of the Scots trumped that of the English. It is conveniently forgotten that before the Wars of Independence around 1300 the relationship of Scotland and England was generally close and often cordial, and that during the wars Robert the Bruce collaborated at times with the English. The powerful image of William Wallace, the hero of the Wars of Independence and of *Braveheart*, was the largely fictional creation of Blind Harry, writing more than 150 years after Wallace's death. In Barbour's more accurate and contemporary account of the Bruce, Wallace does not rate a single mention. In the centuries that followed, Stewarts, clans, Presbyterians, Covenanters, Jacobites and clearances have all been fertile ground for the myth makers.

As the Hollywood maxim has it, 'When the legend becomes fact, print the legend.' I have tried to acknowledge the legend, but I have always attempted to print the fact.

Anyone writing a history of Scotland has to decide what to do about the three centuries since the Union of 1707 with England. Does this mean the end of Scottish history and the start of British? Or is there an awkward appendix after 1707, ending with the Battle of Culloden (1746)? H.E. Marshall, author of *Scotland's Story* (1906), a mawkish romp through Scottish history described by its author as 'a story woven from the golden threads of romance' and by its modern publicists as appealing to 'everyone whose heart stirs at the sound of the bagpipe', ended her account after relating 'how Bonny Prince Charlie came home' and informed her readers that 'The rest of the story of Scotland is the story of the Empire.'

Marshall's book was, of course, the very worst sort of non-history and a classic example of legend prevailing over truth. I have chosen to begin where written record starts and to pursue Scotland's history up to the present, not denying that the nation became part of a United Kingdom, but trying to avoid making the last 300 years a mere catalogue of famous Scots and insisting that Scotland's character and experience were and are distinct from the rest of the UK. In the last decade or two, the redefinition of Scotland's national identity through its artists, writers and filmmakers, and its embodiment in a revived Scottish Parliament, have, I would argue, proved me right. Scotland remains a nation apart.

This book does not pretend to be a complete history of Scotland. There are plenty of good one-volume histories, many of which I have used – Michael Lynch's *Scotland, A New History* (Pimlico, 1995) is the best of the lot. My aim has been rather to give the reader a concise narrative of key events tied to their dates in chronological order. This is not because dates are the be-all and end-all of history – how many of us once suffered in the classroom from being made to learn them by rote? – but because when it comes to the crunch history is also a story, and the sequence of events matters. If you don't know whether Bannockburn came before Flodden, the Covenanters before the Jacobites or Rabbie Burns before David Livingstone then you are at sea without any compass to help you understand the bigger processes of Scottish history – the ups and downs of Anglo-Scottish relations, the emergence of the Kirk, the effect of Union on Scotland's character and institutions, the Enlightenment, the Industrial Revolution and so on.

Once upon a time, the sports pages of Scottish newspapers spoke dismissively of 'Anglos' – Scottish international footballers who played their club football in England. I must confess that when it comes to writing about Scottish history I am an Anglo. I was mostly educated in England and I live there now, as I have done for the last twenty years. But I am half Scottish by birth, have lived in Scotland for much of my life, have many family there and come north every year. Mrs Gunn, a Scottish governess of the old school, taught me to read and write, and Miss Sharpe in Nairn ran, with a rod of iron, the first school I attended. From both of them I absorbed a good deal of what used to be called 'the story of Scotland'; but in writing this book I have discovered how little I really knew. My hope is that it will set a spark in its readers and fire them to find out more.

George Chamier

# AD 80
# THE ROMAN INVASION

Roman general Agricola led a two-pronged expedition up the west and east sides of Caledonia, as the Romans called Scotland, building forts between the Clyde and the Forth. Their advance headquarters was at Inchtuthil on the river Tay.

This is the first date in Scottish history that can be established with certainty. Scotland has been inhabited for at least 10,000 years, but few traces of its people are left from much of that time. They built hill forts, brochs (drystone roundhouses), crannogs (loch dwellings) and they put up standing stones. The remains of some still stand, including world-famous sites such as the neolithic village of Skara Brae on Orkney or the stone circle of Callanish on Lewis. But these folk left nothing in writing. It was only when Scotland made contact with the Romans that Scottish 'recorded' history began.

The British Isles were a long way from Mediterranean civilization, and Scotland was hardly known to the ancient world. The first recorded mention of Britain ('Pretannia') was by a Greek traveller called Pytheas of Marseilles, who described a voyage to northern waters in about 325 BC, but for a long time the islands were seen as beyond the pale of the civilized world.

In 55 BC Julius Caesar led the first Roman invasion of

Britain, though it was not until AD 43 that the Romans settled, and within decades they had incorporated most of southern Britain into their empire. The north was to prove a harder nut to crack.

# 83

# THE FIRST KNOWN BATTLE

The invasion was successful in getting control of southern Scotland for the Romans, but the northern tribes still posed a threat to them. Agricola now launched a major advance north, establishing forts as he went and sending his fleet up the east coast in support. The two armies finally faced each other at a place called Mons Graupius. No one is quite sure where this was – some historians place it in Aberdeenshire, others in Perthshire – but with a change in spelling it later gave its name to the Grampian mountains.

The battle was a major affair: the Roman historian Tacitus, who was married to Agricola's daughter, said that the Caledonian army was 30,000 strong. The Roman army may have been about the same size. He reported the words of the Caledonian leader Calgacus ('swordsman'), the first personal name we know of any Scot, as he addressed his troops before battle:

> You are united. You Caledonians have never been slaves. From here there is no retreat . . . there are no more peoples behind us. There is nothing but rocks and waves, and the Romans are more menacing than them . . . They rob, kill and rape and this they call Roman rule. They make a desert and they call it peace . . . at the very first assault let us show what heroes Caledonia has hidden in her bosom.

Unfortunately these stirring words were probably invented by Tacitus to glamorize his story, and in any case they didn't do their audience much good. The Caledonians were massacred. When battle was joined, the disciplined Roman infantry, led by Agricola himself, proved more than a match for their enemies, and the Roman cavalry threw back the Caledonian charioteers. Then the Romans sent in their reserve cavalry, which broke the Caledonian ranks. It was a rout: 10,000 Caledonians were killed (according to Tacitus), as opposed to 360 Romans. But the remains of the Caledonian army escaped to fight another day and the north of Scotland, although garrisoned in places by Roman troops, never came under Roman rule.

★

**122 Hadrian's Wall.** After Mons Graupius, the Roman fleet sailed round Scotland, but Agricola was recalled to

Rome and the Romans abandoned most of their bases in the north. Skirmishing continued, but the Romans gave up any attempt to conquer Caledonia and add it to their empire. Emperor Hadrian took the decision to defend the empire's northern frontier by building the fortified wall that bears his name, between the Solway and the Tyne.

**143 The Antonine Wall.** Hadrian's Wall effectively deterred any large-scale attacks by the Caledonian tribes, but it did not keep out occasional raiding parties. Irritated by these incursions, Emperor Antoninus Pius ordered a military reoccupation of the Lowlands and the building of a new wall across Scotland's 'waist', between the Clyde and the Forth, with further defensive outposts as far north as the Tay. But within twenty years, the Romans abandoned this new frontier and fell back on Hadrian's Wall.

**150 The First Map of Scotland.** Ptolemy of Alexandria's *Geography* contained the first map to show Scotland, more or less correctly placed and to scale, but canted to the east. Ptolemy also listed the names and territories of a number of tribes in northern Britain, such as the Votadini between the Forth and the Tyne and the Decantae in Easter Ross.

**297 The Painted People.** The first recorded use of the name 'Pict' can be dated to here, derived from the Latin *Picti* – the painted people – to describe the people of Caledonia. This probably referred to the tribes' tattoos or warpaint. Ironically, since they left no written records, we have no idea what the Picts called themselves.

**306 The Romans March North Again.** As the Roman Empire declined, Emperor Constantius Chlorus led an expedition beyond Hadrian's Wall, but was unable to defeat the Caledonians.

**367 'The Conspiracy of the Barbarians'.** This was what Roman historians called the concerted attacks on the empire's frontier by Picts and Scots (confusingly, the latter were settlers from Ireland) who overran Hadrian's Wall in large numbers.

**397 The First Missionary.** St Ninian arrived at Whithorn on the Solway Firth, sent by the Pope to Scotland.

# 410

# THE ROMANS LEAVE

The Roman presence in Scotland, unlike England, where Roman civilization had taken root, was little more than a military occupation. Nevertheless, the withdrawal of Rome's legions left a power vacuum, and the history of the next few centuries in Scotland – called the 'dark ages', since we know so little about them – is one of struggle between the four peoples who occupied the land. The Picts inhabited the north, including the Hebrides north of Ardnamurchan, and the north-east. The Scots, immigrants from Ireland, settled in Dalriada, modern Argyll. In Strathclyde, between the Clyde and the Solway, lived the Romanized Britons. The Borders and Lothian were steadily penetrated by the Angles, Germanic invaders who had taken advantage of Rome's weakness to settle in Britain. In all these regions there were petty kingdoms and chiefdoms that shared a 'heroic' culture of warfare, hunting and feasting, and whose ruling families intermarried as well as fought among themselves and against each other.

# 563

## ST COLUMBA ON IONA

Despite the efforts of St Ninian and the survival of Christianity in the south, Scotland remained mostly pagan. It was not until the arrival from Ireland of twelve missionaries led by St Columba, who founded a monastery on the island of Iona, that conversion became popular. From Iona he took his mission to the Picts, visiting King Bridei at Inverness where he disputed successfully with the Pictish king's pagan priests.

Columba soon gained a reputation as a peacemaker in tribal feuds. He also performed miracles (including the

vanquishing of a monster in Loch Ness) and established churches and monasteries. His influence can be seen in the crosses that from about this era began to appear on Pictish carved stones.

Iona became the centre of a church whose influence spread throughout Scotland and into Northumbria and was ruled not by bishops but by the abbots of monastic villages.

## St Columba

Also known as *Colm Cille* ('Dove of the Church'), Columba was born in Donegal in 522 to an aristocratic family descended from Niall of the Nine Hostages, High King of Ireland. He was educated at the famous monastic school at Clonard Abbey, became a monk and was ordained as a priest. Despite this, he became involved in a feud leading to a battle in which many were killed. He was threatened with excommunication, but allowed instead to go into exile and redeem himself by doing missionary work in Scotland.

No doubt his royal blood helped him gain converts, but he was clearly a man with considerable charisma. As well as being a missionary and organizer he was a scholar, composing hymns and transcribing many books. He died on Iona in 597 and was buried there. The cult of St Columba remained potent long after his death, and the Monymusk reliquary, an eighth-century casket supposedly containing the saint's bones, was carried into battle by Robert the Bruce at Bannockburn in 1314.

★

**604 The Kingdom of Northumbria Founded** by Anglo-Saxon settlers, whose territory included much of south-east Scotland.

**635 The Monastery of Lindisfarne Founded** by monks from Iona.

**664 The Synod of Whitby.** A meeting of churchmen was convened by King Oswiu of Northumbria to decide whether to follow the practices laid down by St Columba or those of the Roman Church. The decision went in favour of Rome, and Columban practices gradually died out in Scotland. This has been regretted ever since by those who believe that 'The Celtic Church gave love, the Roman Church gave law.'

# 685
# DEFEAT OF THE NORTHUMBRIANS

The Northumbrian King Ecgfrith invaded Pictish territory and on 20 May clashed with a Pictish army under King Bridei, son of Beli, at Nechtansmere, near Dunnichen in Angus. Details of the battle are sketchy, but the Picts took advantage of the presence of an area of boggy ground (Dunnichen Moss), where the Northumbrian cavalry were trapped and cut to pieces. Ecgfrith and many of his bodyguard were killed, and his army destroyed. A Pictish

carved stone at Aberlemno, a few miles from Dunnichen, records the battle. This was one of the decisive battles of Scottish history: the power of the Northumbrian Angles never again reached beyond the Forth, thus preserving the independence of most of what was later to become the kingdom of Scotland from what was to become the Anglo-Saxon kingdom of England (the word *sassenach*, used by Scots to describe the English and by Gaels to describe Lowlanders comes from the Gaelic for 'Saxon').

★

**697 The Law of the Innocents.** Lex Innnocentium, set out by St Adomnan, Abbot of Iona, was the Geneva Convention of its day and was endorsed by a number of kings. It was designed to protect women and other non-combatants from the horrors of war.

## Saints

Scotland's dark ages have few written accounts; but what we do know comes from church records and the lives of saints – often semi-legendary and recorded long after. Among the myths can be found the life of St Mungo, the patron saint of Glasgow and its cathedral, who once restored to life a pet robin belonging to St Serf; St Boisel, the first prior of Melrose Abbey, for whom St Boswells is named; St Aidan, an Ionan monk and the founder of Lindisfarne Abbey; St Balfred, the hermit saint of the Bass Rock; St Blane, an apostle of the Picts, whose monastery became the cathedral of Dunblane; St Fillan, who healed the sick, especially the mentally ill, and whose arm emitted a mysterious light; and St Cuthbert, prior of Melrose and later Bishop of Lindisfarne, who performed miracles of healing and lived as a hermit on the Farne Islands, where he protected nesting seabirds.

# 795

# THE VIKINGS RAID IONA

Vikings from Scandinavia began to attack many parts of western Europe at the end of the eighth century. Scotland, just across the North Sea from Denmark and southern Norway, and with similar geography, was an obvious target, and the rich monastery of Iona was a ripe plum for the picking.

At first, the Vikings came in fairly small numbers to plunder and occasionally to trade, but soon great armies arrived, led by jarls (earls) such as Ketil Flatnose and Sigurd the Mighty, intent on carving out new territories

to settle. Most of the Vikings who invaded Scotland were Norwegians, who established permanent colonies in the north and west. The Northern Isles were so thickly settled that they adopted the Norse language: the invasions left Scotland a legacy of words ('bairn', 'flit' and 'brae'), as well as many place names ('firth', 'wick', 'dale').

★

**832 The Birth of the Saltire.** Legend has it that St Andrew promised victory in a dream to the Pictish King Oengus II on the eve of battle against the Angles at Athelstaneford near Haddington. Sure enough, Oengus was victorious after his army saw above the battlefield a white St Andrew's cross formed by clouds against the blue sky. Relics of the saint were allegedly brought to Scotland at some time in the eighth century and housed in the place that was subsequently called St Andrews.

**843 The First King of Scotland**. When the Scot Kenneth MacAlpin ascended the Pictish throne he united the two peoples and was later hailed as the first 'King of Scotland'. Subsequent kings traced their ancestry to him and numbered their reigns from his. However, the truth is less clear cut: although he did establish a dynasty, it is not even certain he was a Scot, and the extent of his realm is unclear since Angles and Vikings ruled over so much of the domain. In addition, Pictish culture persisted for many decades after his death.

**849 St Columba's Shrine.** Kenneth MacAlpin moved St Columba's relics to Dunkeld, making this the most important Christian centre in Scotland.

**878 The Last King of the Picts.** Aed, son of Kenneth MacAlpin, died; the last man to be styled 'King of the Picts'.

**900 The First King of Alba.** Donald II, grandson of Kenneth MacAlpin, died – the first man to be styled 'King of Alba' (the Gaelic for Scotland).

**904 The Battle of Strathearn.** The forces of Alba, led by King Donald II's brother Constantine II, inflicted their first serious defeat on the Vikings. Constantine reigned for forty years and established the integrity of the kingdom of Alba against Viking and Anglo-Saxon pressure. During his reign, the words 'Scotland' and 'Scots' were first used in English sources to describe the kingdom of Alba and its inhabitants.

# 937

## THE FIRST BATTLE WITH THE ENGLISH

When the Viking kingdom of York collapsed, the Scots and Anglo-Saxons confronted each other directly. King Constantine led an army south and the ensuing Battle of Brunanburh pitted the forces of the sixty-year-old Scottish king, including the men of Strathclyde and some Danish allies, against the army of King Athelstan of Wessex, the ruler of most of England. Constantine's invading army was defeated in a great and bloody encounter, which the Anglo-Saxon Chronicle recorded with a triumphal poem. The battle was the first in the many centuries of warfare to come between the 'English' and the 'Scots'.

★

**943 Constantine II Abdicated.** Leaving the throne, he entered a monastery. His long reign established the template of kingship for the next two centuries.

**945 The Gift of Cumbria.** Edward I of England gave Cumbria to Malcolm I in return for help against the Vikings.

**960 The Scots Captured Edinburgh.** The city retained its English name, though – 'the burgh [fort] of Edwin' – after a seventh-century ruler of Northumbria.

**973 Captain Edgar of England.** In a symbolic event, King Edgar of England was rowed on the river Dee at Chester by eight other kings, including Kenneth II, King of Scots. The performance was intended to display Edgar's overlordship of all other British kings, but was used by later English kings to support the false claim that the kings of Scotland owed them allegiance.

**1018 The Battle for Lothian.** Malcolm II defeated an Anglo-Saxon army at Carham, near Coldstream. This battle confirmed the Scots' control of Lothian and set the border with England on the river Tweed. The kings of Scots now ruled virtually the whole area of present-day Scotland, with the exception of Galloway and the regions controlled by Vikings in the north and in the Isles.

**1034 King Duncan Crowned.** To ensure the succession of his grandson Duncan, Malcolm II had arranged the murder of the alternative claimant to the throne, the son of his predecessor Kenneth III.

**1040 Macbeth's Challenge.** Macbeth, Mormaer (regional chief) of Moray, killed King Duncan in battle near Forres, and took the throne.

**1058 Malcolm III Canmore ('Big Head') Became King.** He ruled Scotland for thirty-five years and established a dynasty that lasted for over two centuries. He waged a series of wars against the English in an attempt to gain control of Northumbria, but with little success.

# Macbeth

The historical Macbeth, as opposed to the Shakespearean character, ruled Scotland for seventeen years in relative peace. He certainly gained the throne by slaying a previous king whose name was Duncan (though in battle rather than with a dagger at night), and he did face attack from Siward of Northumbria, who was allied to Duncan's sons, but that is where the similarities end. Duncan was not a good old king, but a rather unsuccessful young one. Macbeth was not a usurper since he had a claim to the throne through his own and his wife's families, and may even have been recognized as king by King Cnut of England in 1031. In any case, acquiring the throne by killing your predecessor was almost normal practice at this time. His wife, Gruoch (Lady Macbeth), is merely a name in the chronicles – we know nothing about her character. No such individuals as Banquo or Macduff are traceable in surviving records. No witches made prophecies to Macbeth and no woods advanced on him. He seems in fact to have been a popular and pious ruler, whose realm was secure enough for him to leave it and visit Rome in 1050. His relations with the English were generally peaceful, but he was involved in frequent warfare against the powerful Thorfinn, Earl of Orkney, who mounted regular raids south in typical Viking style. Macbeth's end came when Malcolm, son of Duncan, invaded in 1057. Macbeth won a battle against him at Lumphanan in Aberdeenshire, but was mortally wounded and died a few days later at Scone.

# St Margaret, 1045–93

Margaret, Scotland's only royal saint, was the daughter of Edward the Exile, the heir to the English throne driven out by the Danish King Cnut after he conquered England. She was born in Hungary, where her father had married a royal princess, and she returned with her family to England as a young woman. After the Norman invasion of 1066, the family fled to Scotland, and in 1072 Margaret married Malcolm Canmore. Margaret bore her husband eight children, including three sons who succeeded him as kings of Scots and a daughter who married Henry I of England.

Known for her devotion to the Church – she attended a midnight service every night and founded the abbey of Dunfermline – and for her care for orphans and the poor, she was canonized in 1251. Margaret was also active in politics, forging relationships between Scotland and Europe, and even England – something that did not make her popular with many Scots. She gave her sons English names (Edgar, Alexander, David) rather than Gaelic ones, and they spent considerable periods at the court of the Anglo-Norman kings.

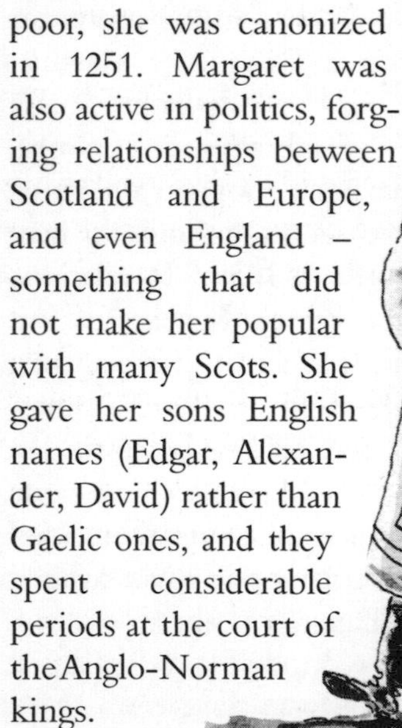

**1066 The Norman Invasion.** Following victory at the Battle of Hastings, William, Duke of Normandy, became King of England. King Malcolm gave asylum to a number of English refugees, including Edgar Aetheling, the legitimate heir to the English throne, and Edgar's sister Margaret. He then made trouble for the Norman king by attacking the north of England while William was occupied in establishing his rule further south.

**1072 William Invaded Scotland.** The Norman king met Malcolm at Abernethy, where the King of Scots was forced to acknowledge the Conqueror's overlordship. This brought peace for a while, but did not stop Malcolm raiding northern England again in the future.

**1093 The Death of King Malcolm.** Malcolm was killed in battle at Alnwick on a final raid into Northumbria.

**1095 The First Crusade.** Relatively few Scots went on crusade in the next two centuries, and those that did tended to be described as 'barbarians' by their fellow crusaders. But the pull of crusading remained strong: when King Robert I lay dying in 1329 he ordered that his heart should be carried on crusade to the Holy Land.

**1097 A Family Feud.** After Malcolm Canmore's death, the crown was fought over by his brother, Donald Bane ('the Fair'), and Duncan, his son by his first marriage. The English intervened frequently in the conflict, and it was with English help that Edgar, the son of Malcolm and Margaret, blinded and deposed Donald Bane.

**1098 The Nation Divided by Boat.** Edgar was forced to acknowledge the rule in the Hebrides of Magnus

'Bare-Legs', King of Norway. It was agreed that the boundary between their respective territories should be the line along which Magnus could travel by boat, but the crafty Norwegian had himself dragged in a longship across the neck of land at Tarbert in Argyll, thus being able to claim the Kintyre peninsula as part of his dominion.

# 1124

## DAVID I, ROYAL REVOLUTIONARY

Both Edgar and his successor Alexander I died childless, so the throne passed to their younger brother David. He was the architect of a new sort of Scottish monarchy, one that greatly expanded royal power and changed the country in many ways. Historians sometimes call this the 'Davidian Revolution'.

Educated in England, David brought many Anglo-Norman governing practices to Scotland: officials such as the chamberlain (finance), the constable (military affairs) and the justiciar (law) became permanent features of the royal household. A Great Council advised the king and approved laws. Sheriffs were appointed to administer law and order in the localities. Burghs (fortified settlements) received royal charters and attracted merchants and craftsmen.

David was the first king of Scots to issue his own coins (the unit was a silver penny, sometimes cut into halves or quarters), and this stimulated industry and trade. New bishoprics were created and monasteries were founded, thus securing the Church's support for the crown. He also brought to Scotland many families from Normandy, Brittany and Flanders (the Bruces and the Stewarts were two of the most celebrated), to whom he granted land in exchange for allegiance and service to the crown. In fact,

## King David I, 1085–1153

David was his father's youngest son, and therefore had little hope of succeeding to the throne. Forced to flee to England with most of his family after his father's death, he stayed there even after his brother Edgar became King of Scots, and was brought up and educated as an Anglo-Norman prince. His sister married King Henry I of England, and so David gained the king's favour, serving him and being granted permission to marry a rich widow who brought him the earldom of Huntingdon and much other English property. During his brother Alexander's reign in Scotland, David ruled Cumbria, where he introduced many of the innovations in government that he would later bring to Scotland, as well as granting lands to his Anglo-Norman friends.

Soon after he became King of Scots, civil war broke out in England between two claimants to the throne, both related to David – his niece Matilda and Stephen, the husband of another niece. David cunningly supported first one and then the other, and →

the Scottish nobility, native and incomer alike, were now bound to serve their king in a feudal system like that of England and France.

★

**1138 The Battle of the Standard.** King David was defeated in Yorkshire, bringing to an end his ambition to push the border further south.

**1153 A Question of Succession.** Malcolm IV, grandson of David I, was just twelve years old, yet his succession succeeded in bringing much of northern England under his rule. His biographer Ailred claimed that David was a ruler of exceptional piety who 'wished to be loved not feared', that he governed justly, tamed the Norsemen and the Gaels, united his people and enriched the land. His career suggests that he was also driven by ruthless ambition and was capable of cynical aggression. His critics have accused him of Anglicizing Scotland. But the new Anglo-Norman lords were invited in (rather than arriving as conquerors, as in Wales and Ireland), and the native aristocracy remained in place, as did many traditional Gaelic customs such as military service. There is no evidence that life for ordinary Scots became any harsher under his rule.

When he died in 1153, King David left Scotland and its crown stronger and richer. He always claimed equality with the kings of England, and he was the first Scottish king to win the respect of his fellow European monarchs. And, however authoritarian his rule may have been, he remained not 'King of Scotland' but the much more personal 'King of Scots'.

was accepted without serious opposition. This also marked the point when lineal descent from the previous king was unquestioningly accepted as the qualification for kingship. Under the former principle of 'tanistry' anyone whose great-grandfather had been a king could claim the throne. Not surprisingly, this had often led to crisis and conflict.

**1157 A New Border.** Malcolm IV gave Northumbria back to the forceful young Henry II of England, whose demands he was unable to resist. The border was fixed on the Solway/Tweed line, close to where it is today.

# 1165
## A LION ON THE THRONE

William I succeeded his unmarried brother Malcolm 'the Maiden' in 1165. He was not known as 'the Lion' in his lifetime; the nickname came not from his powerful build, red hair or headstrong conduct in battle, but from his adoption of a red lion rampant on a yellow background as the royal standard of Scotland (as it remains today). His reign of almost half a century encouraged the process of

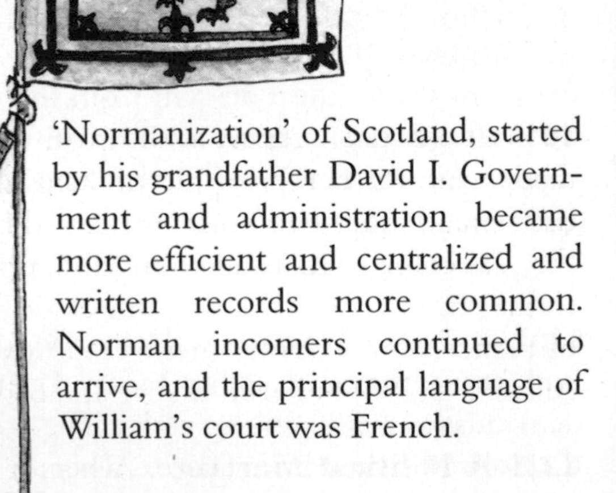

'Normanization' of Scotland, started by his grandfather David I. Government and administration became more efficient and centralized and written records more common. Norman incomers continued to arrive, and the principal language of William's court was French.

★

**1174 The Captured King.** William the Lion joined a revolt against Henry II of England, but was captured in battle at Alnwick and imprisoned at Falaise in Normandy. Henry then promptly invaded Scotland and in exchange for releasing him forced William to sign a treaty acknowledging the King of England as his feudal superior.

**1185 Scotland Bought Back Independence.** William the Lion paid King Richard the Lionheart of England a hefty sum to finance his crusading expedition and was given his independence in return.

**1187 The Death of Donald MacWilliam**, great-grandson of Malcolm Canmore and rebel claimant to the throne, together with the defeat of the MacHeths of Ross, had the effect of pacifying the north, at least temporarily.

**1192 Rome, Not England.** The Pope confirmed that the Scottish Church owed obedience directly to him and was independent of any control by the archbishops of York. The Church in Scotland thus became the 'special daughter' of Rome.

**1216 A Scottish Army in Dover.** Alexander II joined forces with the barons of England against King John, who had reneged on the promises made to them in Magna Carta the year before. He invaded England, marching all the way to the south coast. In Dover Alexander met Prince Louis of France, an encounter that foreshadowed the later 'Auld Alliance' (1295) between France and Scotland.

**1221 A Political Marriage.** Alexander II married Joan,

sister of King Henry III of England. The marriage sealed peace with England that lasted until 1296, the longest such period in the Middle Ages, and was confirmed when Alexander III married Henry III's daughter Margaret in 1251.

**1223 Michael Scot**, medieval Scotland's most famous scholar, was mentioned in a letter from the Pope in this year – the only contemporary written reference to him. Born in the Borders and educated at Oxford and Paris, Scot lived at the brilliant court of Frederick II of Sicily, and wrote on astrology, alchemy and the occult. Dante's *Inferno* included him among the wizards and magicians in the eighth circle of Hell.

**1230 The End of the McWilliam Claim.** The last surviving MacWilliam claimant to the throne, a baby girl, was killed at the order of King Alexander II by having her skull smashed against the market cross in Forfar.

**1233 Building Work Began on Glasgow Cathedral.**

**1235 The First Scottish Parliament.** Later referred to as the Three Estates (clergy, nobility and burghs), the Parliament met at Kirkliston. It played an active role in advising the monarch, approving taxation and passing laws.

**1237 The Border Fixed.** By the Treaty of York the kings of Scots gave up their claim to northern England, and in return were granted lands in Northumbria and Cumbria on condition that they did homage for them to the king of England. This was later used as a pretext by English kings to claim that homage was due for the whole of Scotland too.

**1249 The Stone of Destiny.** The new king, eight-year-old Alexander III, was the first King of Scots whose enthronement was recorded in detail: in accordance with ancient custom he was hailed by a *seanchaidh* or bard, who recited his pedigree in Gaelic, and he was not crowned but 'set on the Stone'. This was the Stone of Destiny, allegedly brought to Scotland by Gaythelus (ancestor of the Gaels), a legendary Greek prince who was supposedly married to Scota, an Egyptian princess.

**1263 The Battle of Largs.** King Haakon of Norway, aided by the Earl of Orkney, the King of Man and various Hebridean chieftains, led a great expedition to assert his overlordship of the Western Isles. Alexander III defeated Haakon in battle on 2 October and in a subsequent campaign made himself overlord of the Western Isles and the Isle of Man.

**1266 The Departure of the Norwegians.** Norway gave up its claims to all Scottish territory except Orkney and Shetland by the Treaty of Perth.

## The Lords of the Isles

The Norwegian Vikings who settled on the west coast and in the Hebrides after 800 intermarried with the local Gaels and founded a kingdom of *Gall-Gaidheal* ('Foreign Gaels'), from which the name Galloway originates. The Lords of the Isles, as their rulers were known, gave nominal allegiance to the kings of Norway or kings of Scots, but in practice were mostly independent of either, their power based on remoteness and command of the sea. They were forced on the defensive at times, but were quick to take advantage when the Scottish crown was weak. Sometimes the lordship was divided, but the great Somerled in the twelfth century ruled lands stretching from the Isle of Man to the Butt of Lewis. Later the Macdonald family became Lords of the Isles, and the chiefs of Clan Donald in the fourteenth and fifteenth centuries ruled territories as great as Somerled's, but in 1493 John Macdonald finally submitted to the crown.

'Lord of the Isles' became a title granted by the crown instead of being assumed as of right, and was then taken over by the kings of Scots and granted to their male heir. Thus the present Lord of the Isles is Prince Charles.

**1286 The Maid of Norway.** Hurrying home to see his new wife, Alexander III fell from his horse at Kinghorn in Fife and was killed. The king's death left his country in a dangerous position: he had no living children, and his only direct heir was his three-year-old granddaughter, the Maid of Norway, born to his daughter Margaret who had married the Norwegian King Eric II.

**1290 An Infant Wedding.** By the Treaty of Birgham the Guardians of Scotland, appointed to govern after Alexander's death agreed that the Maid of Norway should marry the two-year-old Prince Edward, heir to the English throne. Unfortunately, the little girl fell ill and died in Orkney on her way back to Scotland.

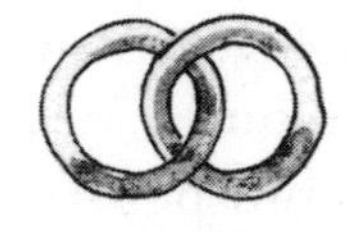

# 1291

# THE GREAT CAUSE

The death of the Maid of Norway presented King Edward I of England, who had already conquered Wales, with the chance he had been looking for to add Scotland to his empire. The Guardians of Scotland made the mistake of asking Edward to choose Scotland's new king, and this gave him the opportunity to act in the 'Great Cause' as if he was Scotland's feudal overlord. No fewer than thirteen competitors for the Scottish throne came forward, but there were only two serious ones, both direct descendants of David I: John Balliol and Robert Bruce.

After a lengthy judicial process in front of a jury of 104 men, Balliol was chosen as king, and he then performed homage for the kingdom before Edward, recognizing publicly that the English king was his superior. In fact, he was treated so patronizingly by Edward that he acquired the derisive nickname 'Toom Tabard' (Empty Coat).

★

**1295 The Auld Alliance Launched.** When King Edward demanded men and money from Scotland for his French war, King John Balliol, spurred on by Parliament, decided he had had enough. A Scottish delegation sailed for France and signed an alliance, which gave little help to Scotland but was effectively a declaration of war against England. The Scots knew what was coming next, and the army was mustered in preparation.

# 1296
## THE WAR OF INDEPENDENCE

King Edward's nickname, 'the Hammer of the Scots', was earned in brutal style. His first step was to sack Berwick and massacre many of its inhabitants. He then crushed the Scottish army at Dunbar and continued to march north, reaching the Moray Firth. As a result, King John was forced to abdicate and dispatched with many Scottish nobles into captivity in England. The Stone of Scone was taken south to Westminster Abbey. Government records were removed, an oath of loyalty to Edward was demanded from leading Scots, and English viceroys were appointed to govern Scotland for its new overlord.

The message was clear: Scotland's independence was at an end. But King Edward had reckoned without the determined spirit of his adversaries. His arrogant and harsh treatment of them merely kindled a defiant patriotism, which meant that the rest of his life was occupied with largely unsuccessful attempts to make good his claim to rule Scotland.

★

**1297 Wallace Rampant.** Within months of Balliol's abdication, rebellions against English rule had broken out in various parts of the country. Two rebel leaders, Andrew de Moray and William Wallace, linked up and caught the English army crossing Stirling Bridge on 11 September. They inflicted a heavy defeat on the enemy due to the effective manoeuvring of the Scottish 'schiltrons', close-packed formations of spearmen who did terrible damage to the English mounted knights.

**1298 Edward's Retaliation**. King Edward returned to seek revenge for Stirling Bridge, and at Falkirk on 22 July his Welsh archers turned the tables and put the schiltrons to flight. Wallace survived, however, and began a hugely successful campaign of guerrilla warfare.

**1303 King Edward on the Offensive.** After an inconclusive invasion in 1300, Edward's army, which remained in Scotland during the winter of 1303/4, took Stirling, the last Scots stronghold, and forced most of the Scottish nobility to submit. William Wallace, however, remained defiant and at liberty.

## William Wallace, 1270–1305

Hard facts about Wallace are difficult to come by, for his life is very poorly documented. He was the younger son of an obscure Clydesdale laird, and his first act of resistance against King Edward's rule was the killing of the English sheriff of Lanark in 1297. His rapid emergence as a leader at the stunning victory of Stirling Bridge led to his knighthood and appointment as 'Guardian and Leader of the Armies of Scotland'. Even defeat at the Battle of Falkirk did not damage his reputation, since it stiffened the resolve of many Scots to continue resisting the English.

After Falkirk, Wallace resigned the Guardianship to Robert Bruce and John Comyn and sailed to France to drum up support for the Scottish cause. Before he left, he had shown the way forward by adopting guerrilla tactics to harry the English, including a devastating raid into Northumberland; he had also ensured that the Scottish Church gave its continuing moral support to the cause of independence.

He returned in 1303 and took part in resistance to King Edward's campaigns of 1303/4, but in 1305 he was captured by a Scottish knight loyal to King Edward and taken to London. After a show trial in Westminster Hall (Wallace refused to acknowledge the charge of →

**1304 John Duns Scotus**, the celebrated philosopher and theologian who taught at both Oxford and Cambridge, was appointed to the University of Paris, then at the height of its intellectual supremacy. To some he was known as 'Doctor Subtilis' for his skilful blending of different schools of philosophy, but critics used his name 'Duns' treason since, he said, he had never been a subject of the English king), he was stripped naked and dragged through the streets to Smithfield, where he was hanged, drawn and quartered. His head was then put on a pike at London Bridge, and other body parts were displayed in various cities in Scotland and northern England.

Wallace's brief career made him the national hero of the War of Independence, and the manner of his death made him a martyr for the cause. Since his death, a mass of stories and legends have grown up around him, mostly based on the 1470 account of his life by the minstrel-poet Blind Harry and given fresh impetus in our own times by the film *Braveheart.* We should separate myth from reality, though. For example, Wallace was definitely not a 'man of the people'. He may have been the champion of a popular cause, but no common man could have attracted the support of noblemen, as he did, let alone been appointed Guardian of Scotland. Behind the myth, however, there was a remarkable leader and a brave man, whose refusal to submit to alien rule inspired his fellow Scots to fight to the death for their independence.

(from his birthplace in the Borders) to insult his followers as 'dunces'.

**1306 Robert the Bruce Claimed the Throne.** The Comyn and Bruce families had a history of enmity, and the two men had been uneasy allies against the English. Both had surrendered to King Edward in 1304, but John Comyn ('the Red') refused to support Bruce's desire to revive the war. Bruce killed Comyn at a meeting in a church, and declared himself king at Scone. The murder shocked the nation, caused Bruce to be excommunicated by the Pope and turned the powerful Comyn family and their allies against the new King Robert.

**1307 The Death of Edward I.** The English king swore 'before God and the swans' (royal birds that had just been presented to him when he heard the news) to avenge Comyn and marched north, but fortunately for Scotland he died en route. When Edward II succeeded his father on the English throne, King Robert's fortunes began to change: he defeated his enemies at home, recaptured most of the English-held castles, mounted successful raids into England and used effective guerrilla tactics against the occupying English armies. As a result, support rallied to him and he gained the trust of the people.

# 1314

## THE BATTLE OF BANNOCKBURN

In 1310 Edward II, brave but lacking the forceful generalship of his father, led an invasion of Scotland. King Robert avoided confrontation, however, and the English army achieved little. Edward came back in force four years later, determined to lift the siege of Stirling, the last substantial stronghold in English hands, and confront the Scots on the battlefield. He got his wish beside the Bannock Burn, near Stirling, where his army of about 20,000 men met a Scottish force of less than half that size.

The Scots were ready for him, positioned on higher ground and screened by trees, above a marshy plain through which the burn flowed. In front of them they had dug concealed pits and traps. Initial English attacks were repulsed, and then an incident occurred that was straight out of a romance, yet completely true: an English knight, Henry de Bohun, spotted King Robert and charged him, lance at the ready, thinking to win glory for himself and decapitate the Scots' army before battle was joined. Robert, mounted on a small and agile pony, dodged his opponent and, as the heavily armoured knight thundered past, rose in the saddle and brought his battleaxe down on Bohun's helmet, shearing through metal and bone and killing him with a single blow.

On the next day, 24 June, the battle began in earnest, with

a charge by the English cavalry, but they got stuck in the boggy ground and concealed traps, and the struggling mass of men and horses got in the way of the English archers. This was the cue for the Scottish spearmen, trained to manoeuvre in formation, to fall on their opponents, who began to retreat. 'Lay on! They fail!' was the cry, and the schiltrons, backed up by a charge of Highlanders, utterly routed the enemy.

English casualties were enormous, many prisoners were taken and the ransoms and booty pumped a huge sum into Scottish coffers. Bannockburn was a victory based on meticulous training, high morale and disciplined leadership. It was not the end of the war, but it was the decisive event in the eventual defeat of English attempts to conquer their neighbours. The battle is recalled in Scotland's unofficial anthem, 'Flower of Scotland'.

★

**1315–18 Famine.** Starvation was rarely far away for the poor, and famines were often recorded by the chroniclers. Three successive harvest failures led to a particularly severe one in these years.

# 1320
# THE DECLARATION OF ARBROATH

After Bannockburn, no English armies troubled Scotland for some time. Instead, King Robert took the opportunity to ravage northern England and sent an army to open a second front against the English in Ireland. Yet one enemy he could not defeat: the Pope had taken England's side because the Scottish king was still excommunicated for the murder of John Comyn. So Abbot Bernard of Arbroath was commissioned to compose an appeal to the Pope to recognize Scotland's independence. The Declaration of Arbroath, which vies with the National Covenant (1638) as the most famous document of Scottish history, spoke humbly of 'this poor little Scotland, beyond which there is no dwelling place at all', but closed with these stirring words:

> As long as a hundred of us remain alive, we will never under any condition be subjected to the lordship of the English. For we fight not for glory, riches or honour, but for freedom alone, which no good man gives up except with his life.

Another section of the Declaration has often been taken to be an early expression of the stubbornly egalitarian Scottish character and the refusal of Scots to respect authority merely for its own sake:

> Yet if [King Robert] should give up what he has begun, seeking to make us or our kingdom subject to the King of England, we would strive at once to drive him out as our enemy.

## Robert the Bruce, 1274–1329

The man who would secure Scotland's independence was born a member of the Norman family de Brus, originally brought in – like so many others – by King David I, and granted extensive lands in Annandale. Bruce had true Scottish blood too, since he was also descended from King Malcolm Canmore, and his mother's family was of the old Gaelic nobility. Bruce's grandfather, 'the Competitor', claimed the throne in 1291 but lost out to John Balliol. The Bruce family never gave up their belief that they were the rightful heirs to the throne of Scotland.

In 1296, Robert joined Edward I against Balliol, but in the next two years he changed sides twice, joining William Wallace before returning to Edward and then becoming Guardian along with John Comyn in 1298. In 1302 and 1304 he again swore allegiance to Edward before taking the biggest gamble of his life – the murder of his rival Comyn and the seizure of the throne. It looked as if the gamble had failed, since he suffered a series of military defeats and was forced to flee to the West Highlands (this is when he is supposed to have watched a spider doggedly spinning its web across a cave and drawn the lesson that he must 'try, try and try again').

His luck turned when Edward I died in 1307, →

and in the following years he led a brilliantly successful guerrilla campaign against the English. The subsequent victory at Bannockburn crowned his military achievements, finally establishing his throne and enabling him to raid England at will. In his last years, the Treaty of Edinburgh/Northampton and recognition by the Pope set the seal on his success.

After his death his heart was taken on crusade, as he had wished, by Sir James Douglas and reached the front line of the war against the Moors in Spain before being brought back for burial at Melrose Abbey.

Robert the Bruce was a less glamorous figure than William Wallace and less attractive to the myth makers, since his life was better documented, including by Barbour's 1375 poem *The Brus* ('A! Fredome is a noble thing'). He is rightly remembered as the liberator of the nation, and he left an ordered kingdom to his son and heir, but unfortunately that heir – something that would recurrently plague Scotland in the next two centuries – was a five-year-old boy.

★

**1328 A Temporary Peace.** Edward III of England had succeeded his father the year before, and the new young king signed the Treaty of Edinburgh/Northampton, which arranged the betrothal of his little sister to King Robert's son David, recognized the independence of Scotland, fixed the border and acknowledged the right of the Bruce dynasty to the throne. But Edward signed with his fingers crossed, as would soon be discovered.

**1329 The Excommunication Revoked.** The Pope acknowledged the independence of Scotland by revoking the excommunication of Robert and giving his permission for future kings of Scots to be anointed and formally crowned. In the same year, King Robert died.

**1332 The Return of the Balliols.** Robert's son David II succeeded in peace in 1329, but it was not long before his enemies attempted to oust him. Edward Balliol, son of King John, and other Scots nobles who had been 'disinherited' by the Bruces, assembled an army in England with the connivance of King Edward III and launched an invasion. They soundly defeated the Earl of Mar, Guardian of Scotland, at Dupplin Moor, near Perth, and Edward Balliol had himself crowned king. The second War of Independence had begun.

**1333 The Revenge for Bannockburn.** Edward Balliol acknowledged the overlordship of King of Edward III of England, who now invaded Scotland to make good his claim to the south, which Balliol had agreed to hand over to him. At Halidon Hill, near Berwick, the English army inflicted a crushing defeat on the Scots under their new Guardian, Archibald Douglas. Many Englishmen saw the battle as 'revenge for Bannockburn', and the surviving Scottish nobles sent the young King David into exile in France for safety.

**1341 The Return from Exile.** After Halidon Hill, English armies systematically ravaged Scotland, but men loyal to King David mounted a guerrilla campaign that restricted the rule of Balliol to a small area of the south-west. By the time King David returned, Balliol had fled.

**1346 The Capture of the King.** King David led a rash invasion of England and was defeated and captured at Neville's Cross in County Durham. He was taken to London and imprisoned in the Tower. In David's absence, his nephew Robert Stewart acted as regent.

**1350 The Black Death**. In 1349 Scots had rejoiced when England was hit by the plague, which they saw as God's punishment for the sins of the English. Scotland suffered relatively lightly, losing perhaps a quarter of its population as against a third or more in England.

**1356 The Burnt Candlemas.** This was the name given to Edward III's devastation of Lothian in February, the most savage of his campaigns across the border.

**1357 The King's Ransom.** In the Treaty of Berwick Edward agreed to release King David in return for an enormous ransom of 100,000 merks (more than £60,000 sterling). This was a huge sum for a poor country to raise, and David considered selling the succession to the Scottish throne to Edward in return for remission of the debt. But Parliament refused to allow it, and three-quarters of the sum was eventually paid, at the cost of draining Scotland of silver, leaving a debased currency and a devastated economy.

# 1371

## THE RISE OF THE STEWARTS

King David II's reign was unimpressive. He spent much of it in exile or captivity, had little military success against the English, impoverished his land and almost sold the throne to King Edward. In addition, a bitter Anglo-Scottish enmity became entrenched on both sides of the border.

David died childless and was succeeded in 1371 by Robert II, the son of his sister Marjorie by her marriage to Walter, the high steward. Walter's position at court was a hereditary role given in the twelfth century by David I to a Breton family, who later adopted the title as their surname. The Stewart dynasty – spelled 'Stuart' by Mary, Queen of Scots, from the mid-sixteenth century, to ensure the French pronounced it properly – ruled Scotland, and later England too, more or less continuously for the next 344 years.

★

**1372 Scotland Exported 1,500 Tons of Wool.** This made it second only to England among European wool-exporting countries.

**1378 The Great Schism**. A rival Pope was established under French protection in Avignon. In line with the Auld Alliance, Scotland recognized him as the legitimate pontiff.

## The Auld Alliance

It has been said that the Auld Alliance was a matter of 'warriors, women, writers and wine'. With respect to the first two, the formal relationship between Scotland and France began with the 1295 treaty against their mutual enemy, the English. In practice, the alliance was rarely helpful to Scotland in a direct military way: the French gave little aid during the Wars of Independence, and when a French army did arrive in 1385, they proved unpopular with the locals and found their hosts to be unwelcoming and uncivilized.

However, a considerable contingent of Scots went to France to fight the English in the Hundred Years' War, especially after the Battle of Agincourt (1415), and some were granted French titles and estates. The foremost French general of the Italian wars around 1500 was Bernard Stuart d'Aubigny, a member of the Stewart family of Darnley, who employed many Scottish soldiers in his armies. The kings of France kept a permanent elite corps of Scots, the Garde Écossaise, as their bodyguard.

Marriages between the two royal families helped cement the alliance, in particular the marriage of James V to Mary of Guise in 1538. Their daughter was Mary, Queen of Scots, who married the dauphin and became briefly also Queen of France. For a time it looked as though the crowns of Scotland and France would be united. But the Treaty of Edinburgh (*see* 1560) brought the alliance to an end, after Scotland became a Protestant country and an English invasion chased out the occupying French.

The Auld Alliance was as much about culture as high politics. Many Scots studied at French universities, →

and Scottish universities were consciously modelled on the French pattern. Many Scottish scholars had their works first published in France, and the first Scottish printers learned their trade there. Scots looked to France for instruction in art, architecture and literature, and aristocrats saw it as the source of finery and civilized living. French words entered the Scots language, such as 'gigot' for a shoulder of lamb, 'ashet' (*assiette*) for a big plate, even 'loo' as in '*gardez l'eau*', the cry before a chamber pot was emptied into the Edinburgh streets from an upper window.

French wine was the drink of choice for all who could afford it; there was a colony of Scottish wine merchants in Bordeaux, and in 1539 it was recorded that Cardinal Beaton stocked his cellars with more than 100,000 bottles. The formal alliance ended in 1560, but the friendship persists to this day, as anyone can see when France and Scotland encounter each other on the rugby field in Edinburgh or Paris.

**1380 Scottish Merchants Settled in Gdansk (Danzig)**, trading in furs, leather, cloth and grain, the start of a long-lasting commercial connection with the Baltic region. Others settled in cities such as Warsaw and Krakow, and by about 1600 there may have been as many as 30,000 Scottish families in the region. A medieval French proverb declared, 'Rats, lice and Scotsmen: you find them the whole world over,' an oblique tribute to the Scots' enduring tendency to leave their homeland as soldiers, pilgrims, students, scholars and businessmen.

## King and Barons

The behaviour of the Wolf of Badenoch (*see* 1390) was an extreme example of a problem faced by the kings of Scots – how to deal with powerful and unscrupulous barons. King Robert II had more than twenty children, over half of them legitimate, and lived well into his seventies. His adult sons were among those noblemen who maintained private armies, indulged in vendettas, competed for wealth and power and rebelled against the crown.

After Robert III the next six monarchs came to the throne as minors, which gave ambitious nobles the opportunity to make trouble. This was also the time that a sharp division began to open between Lowlands and Highlands: the Wolf of Badenoch's men were called 'wild wikked Hielandmen', and the Gaelic-speaking Highland *caterans* (marauders) were described as 'a savage and untamed race, rude and independent, given to rapine and exceedingly cruel'. When trouble came, it often originated in the north, and many Highland clansmen and their chiefs lived outside the effective reach of the king's law.

**1388 The Battle of Otterburn.** A Scottish army under James, Earl of Douglas defeated the English forces led by Henry Percy, 'Harry Hotspur'. Douglas did not survive his victory, and a famous ballad described his dream on the eve of battle: 'I saw a dead man win a fight, and I knew that man was I.'

**1390 The 'Wolf of Badenoch'.** A few months after his father's death, Alexander Stewart, the fourth son of King Robert II, attacked Elgin and burned its cathedral. The act might have been the beginning of a bid for the throne or the settling of a private quarrel, but was typical of the atrocious behaviour of the 'Wolf of Badenoch', who had long conducted a reign of terror across the Highlands. He is supposed to have met his end soon afterwards, when he rashly challenged the devil at chess.

**1396 The Battle of the North Inch.** A feud between Clan Chattan and Clan Kay was settled by a set-piece battle at Perth, thirty men a side, and witnessed by the king, many nobles and invited foreign visitors. Only a dozen of

the sixty fighters survived, but eleven of them were Chattans, so they had the victory.

**1400 Another English Invasion.** This was the last time a king of England in person led an army across the border and although Henry IV achieved little, a Scottish army did suffer defeat two years later at Homildon Hill, the last battle of any size between Scots and English until Flodden in 1513. The following century was one of wary cold war with only occasional outbreaks of violence. As a visitor to the court of James I in 1430 remarked, 'nothing pleases the Scots more than abuse of the English.'

**1406 The Kidnap of the Prince.** King Robert III was disabled in a riding accident, and real power passed into the hands of his brother, the Duke of Albany. When Robert's elder son died in mysterious circumstances, probably at Albany's hands, the king sent his ten-year-old surviving son and heir James to France for safety – but the prince was captured by English pirates and handed over to the authorities. King Robert died soon after receiving the news, and James remained in captivity, while Albany continued to govern Scotland.

**1411 The Battle of Red Harlaw.** Near Inverurie an army sent by Albany confronted a Highland horde, including several thousand Irish mercenaries known as *gallowglasses* (foreign warriors), led by Donald Macdonald, Lord of the Isles. In the confusion of battle, both sides claimed victory, although Clan Donald's advance was halted.

**1413 The University of St Andrews** was founded, followed by Glasgow in 1451, Aberdeen in 1495 and Edinburgh in 1582, at which time England still had only two universities – Oxford and Cambridge. Aberdeen got a second university (Marischal College) in 1593.

**1424 'A King Unleashed'.** James I was released from his long captivity in England in exchange for a large ransom and a number of hostages. While in the south he had married a cousin of the English king Henry VI, developed his considerable skills at jousting and music and wrote *The Kingis Quair* (*The King's Book*), a long semi-autobiographical poem. Back in Scotland, he threw himself energetically into the business of government, introducing new taxes and passing many laws. He also executed all the male members of the Albany family and their allies, just in case.

**1437 The Murder of the King.** James I's strong government upset some of his subjects, and a plot was hatched by descendants of his grandfather Robert II's first marriage, who believed they had a better claim to the throne. James tried to escape his assassins by climbing through a sewer, but they caught him underground and stabbed him to death. His death was instantly avenged when his killers were brutally tortured and executed, and his six-year-old son James succeeded peacefully to the throne.

**1440 The Black Dinner.** The regents of Scotland, fearing the influence of the powerful Douglas family, invited the Earl of Douglas and his brother to dine with the young king in Edinburgh. At the table a black bull's head was brought in, and afterwards the Douglases were dragged out, given a mock trial and executed.

**1446 Rosslyn Chapel Founded** by the Earl of Caithness. It was built as a collegiate chapel or chantry to offer prayers for the dead. It is full of cryptic carvings and decoration supposedly connected with the Knights Templar and the Freemasons, if you are willing to believe *The Da Vinci Code.*

**1449 A Marriage with Burgundy.** The marriage between James II and Mary of Gueldres, niece of the Duke of Burgundy and its glittering celebration at Holyrood did much to raise the status of the kingdom of Scotland on the European stage. The young king appeared slim and elegant in black, despite the red birthmark that completely covered one cheek (he was known as 'James of the Fiery Face').

**1455 James II Protected his Throne.** The crown had come to fear the power of the Douglas family, the sometimes loyal lieutenants of the kings of Scots. At Stirling, therefore, James dealt with the problem himself and struck the first blow with his own dagger against the Eighth Earl of Douglas.

**1457 Golf Banned.** James II decreed that football and golf be banned in order to encourage archery practice. Later monarchs enjoyed golf, however: Mary, Queen of Scots is said to have played on the links at Seton House a few days after the murder of her husband Darnley in 1567, while James VI gave his royal warrant to an Edinburgh clubmaker in 1603 and took his clubs south with him when he travelled to England to become king.

**1460 James II Killed.** The king was an artillery enthusiast: he acquired through his wife's family the enormous gun known as Mons Meg, now at Edinburgh Castle, and used cannon effectively in his campaigns against the Douglases. At the siege of Roxburgh, one of the last border strongholds held by the English, James was killed when a nearby cannon exploded.

**1468 Orkney and Shetland Became Scottish.** The young King James III was betrothed to the daughter of the King of Norway, and the islands were part of her dowry. However, their culture remained as much Norse as Scottish, as it still is today.

**1472 St Andrews Became an Archbishopric**, thus increasing the dignity of the Scottish Church and the status of Scotland in Christendom. Glasgow followed in 1492.

**1482 Berwick Lost Forever.** Over the centuries the border town had changed hands a dozen times but it was finally lost when James III faced an English-sponsored rebellion by his brother Alexander. Nevertheless, its football team has always played in the Scottish leagues.

**1488 The Battle of Sauchieburn.** James III was confronted by an army of disgruntled nobles, including his own son. The nobility saw him as harsh, devious and suspiciously pro-English. After a skirmish at Sauchieburn, near Stirling, the king was killed while trying to escape from the battlefield.

**1496 The Education Act.** Parliament passed a law

## James IV, 1473–1513

Only fifteen when he came to the throne, James rapidly established himself as a colourful personality and a formidable ruler. He deeply regretted his part in his father's death and wore an iron chain round his waist as a penance for the rest of his life, but sensibly did not take revenge on anyone involved.

He was a Renaissance prince, interested in everything from ships, guns and jousting to music, clothes and architecture, and was a notable patron of the arts and sciences. He practised medicine and spoke a number of languages. Nor did he neglect his administrative duties. He called regular Parliaments, appointed good counsellors and reformed the system of justice. He travelled his kingdom incessantly, meeting ordinary people and convincing them of his care for the poor. Highlanders were impressed by his ability to speak Gaelic, and he brought relative peace to the outlying parts of the kingdom in the north, the west and the Borders. He reformed the army and navy, building the *Great Michael* – at 1,000 tons the biggest warship in Europe, almost twice the size of Henry VIII's *Mary Rose*.

making it compulsory for all those involved in giving justice (i.e. landowners) to send their sons to school.

**1497 A Chair Of Medicine.** A professor of medicine was appointed at Aberdeen University, the first at any university in Scotland or England.

**1490 The Fairy Flag of the Clan MacLeod** was waved during a fight with the Macdonalds at Trumpan on Skye

and allegedly turned the course of the battle. The flag, still on display at Dunvegan Castle, is said to have one magically effective wave left in it – Dame Flora MacLeod, the twenty-eighth chief of the clan, offered to wave it over the cliffs of Dover during the Battle of Britain in 1940, but her offer was politely refused.

**1498 The Shore Porters Society Founded**, as a cooperative for mutual protection by a group of porters at Aberdeen harbour. The society is still trading as a removals and haulage company today.

**1499 The Death of Robert Henryson.** One of the great figures of this golden age of Scottish poetry, Henryson wrote in Scots, as it was now called (rather than 'Inglis', as previously), which was also now the language of government. His narrative poems such as the *Fables* were based on scenes of everyday life and combined a light touch with serious moral purpose.

**1503 The Marriage of the Thistle and the Rose.** James IV married Margaret Tudor, daughter of King Henry VII of England. The marriage, celebrated in Dunbar's poem 'The Thrissil and the Rois', was hailed as a 'union of hearts' and came with a Treaty of Perpetual Peace between the old enemies. Princess Margaret, not yet fourteen at the time of the wedding, bore six children. Exactly a hundred years after the marriage, the couple's great-grandson James VI united the crowns of England and Scotland.

**1504 The Eskdale Raid and 'Jeddart Justice'.** James led a successful attack on Border reivers (cattle rustlers), and at Jedburgh his prisoners were treated to an extreme form of summary justice – hanged first, tried afterwards.

**1505 'Lament for the Makaris' Published.** William Dunbar was the second of the great makars (poets) of the age and in this poem he recalled those who had gone before him. The poem is in Scots, but each verse ends with the forbidding line in Latin, *Timor mortis conturbat me* ('The fear of death distresses me'). Dunbar's verse was often sharply satirical, and although he was a Franciscan friar his poems contained the first use in print of two well-known four-letter obscenities beginning with 'f' and 'c'.

**1507 A Tournament at Holyrood.** The three-day event was typical of James' flamboyant, cosmopolitan court. He understood the importance of display in cultivating an image of himself as a Renaissance prince, with buildings such as Holyrood Palace and the magnificent Great Hall at Stirling Castle and his patronage of the arts. At the tournament James personally beat knights from Denmark, England and France, in defence of a mysterious 'black lady'. Events such as this served to unite the nobility behind their king and encouraged them to follow him when war came.

**1508 The First Book Printed** in Scotland by Walter Chepman and Andrew Myllar in Edinburgh was Lydgate's *Complaint of the Black Knight.* Only twenty books printed in Scotland before 1540 have survived, and many Scottish scholars continued to have their works printed in Paris.

**1513 *Eneados***, the first translation into any form of English of Virgil's *Aeneid*, was completed by Gavin Douglas. After Henryson and Dunbar, Douglas was the third of the great figures of the Scots literary renaissance, but he produced no further verse after the Battle of Flodden.

# 1513

## THE BATTLE OF FLODDEN

Flodden was the worst defeat ever suffered by a Scottish army at the hands of the English. Under James IV, relations with England were generally good and reached a peak when James married Princess Margaret and signed 'perpetual peace' with the old enemy. But all this changed when Henry VII died in 1509 and the young Henry VIII went to war against France. The Auld Alliance drew Scotland into the fray on the French side, despite James' best efforts to avoid conflict. He eventually led his army across the border while Henry was occupied in France.

On 9 September he met the English, under the Earl of Surrey, a few miles south of the Tweed near Branxton in Northumberland. Each force was about 20,000 men strong and the Scots held a potential advantage on higher ground. However, this positionallowed

the English artillery to pick them off, while the Scots were unable to reply in kind since their best guns were with the fleet. When battle was joined, the Scottish schiltrons with their long pikes were ineffective on the muddy ground against the more manoeuvrable English formations with shorter and handier halberds.

Even if English claims of 10,000 Scottish dead were an exaggeration, there is no doubt that it was a massacre. King James himself was slain, the last monarch to die in battle in the British Isles, as were nine earls, thirteen barons and many other noblemen. It was said that every noble family in Scotland lost someone at Flodden. The dead were remembered in the haunting song and bagpipe tune, 'The Flowers of the Forest', who 'are all wede [withered] away'.

★

**1513 The Regency.** The new king, James V, was not yet eighteen months old, and his regency would be marked by squabbles, which occasionally erupted into open violence between various relations of the little king, pro-French and pro-English factions and noble families, especially the Douglases and the Hamiltons. The queen dowager added to the confusion when she married Archibald Douglas, Earl of Angus – a marriage that produced Henry, Lord Darnley, the second husband of Mary, Queen of Scots. The queen later divorced Angus and scandalized Scotland by marrying a third husband many years her junior.

**1521 John Mair's *History of Greater Britain***, the first printed history of Scotland, was published, in which Mair argued for an eventual union of Scotland with England.

**1525 An Act Against 'Heretical Literature'.** This was a vain attempt to stop the spread of Protestant doctrines that before long would take root in Scotland.

**1527 Hector Boece's *History of the Scottish People*.** This was a lively and patriotic account, if not an entirely accurate one. It was on Boece's description of Macbeth that Shakespeare based his largely fictional character.

**1528 James V's Personal Rule.** The pro-English party, led by his stepfather's family, made young James a virtual prisoner, but at the age of sixteen he escaped and asserted himself as king, taking savage revenge on his captors: his stepfather's sister was burned to death for alleged treason. He then established himself as a forceful ruler, taxing his subjects heavily, taking a strong line against religious dissent and attending conscientiously to the business of government. Red-haired and hot-tempered, he also had considerable charm. He was known as the 'gaberlunzie' (wandering beggar) king from his habit of going about among his people in disguise, and he had an eye for the girls, conducting numerous affairs and fathering at least nine children.

**1528 The Martyrdom of Patrick Hamilton.** Scotland's first Protestant martyr was burned at the stake in St Andrews. The fire took six hours to consume his body.

**1530 James V's Border Campaign.** The king took on the lords of the Borders, temporarily pacifying this troublesome region. Ten years later he tackled the Highlands, sailing round the coast from Edinburgh to Dumbarton and receiving the submissions of many chiefs.

**1532 The Court of Session Founded**, the supreme court for civil cases in Scotland.

**1538 James V Married Mary of Guise.** One of Europe's most eligible bachelors, James played the diplomatic marriage game skilfully, and after a lengthy stay at the French court he opted for a dynastic alliance with France. His first marriage, to Madeleine, daughter of King Francis I, only lasted months, but after her death he quickly married Mary of Guise, whom Henry VIII of England also had his eye on as his fourth wife. Both of James' French brides brought colossal dowries with them, which helped to finance his lavish court and his ambitious building programme at the palaces of Stirling and Falkland.

**1539 The Scottish Crown Was Remodelled**, using gold mined at Crawford Muir near Biggar.

**1541 Curling.** This year saw the first mention of the game of curling, which was generally seen as the most typical of Scottish sports before golf and football took its place.

# 1542

# THE BATTLE OF SOLWAY MOSS

King James V's French marriage annoyed Henry VIII, his uncle. He also refused to follow the English king in renouncing the authority of Rome over the Church. When James failed to turn up for a planned meeting at York the furious Henry sent an army north to punish his nephew. The English were defeated at Haddon Rig in Teviotdale, but the Scottish counterattack ended disastrously on 24 November at Solway Moss near the river Esk.

In an uncoordinated and shambolic battle the Scots were defeated by a much smaller English force, and although casualties were light, the English succeeded in taking more than a thousand prisoners. Just a week later James died at Falkirk, probably from dysentery or cholera rather than a 'broken heart', as is often alleged.

History now repeated itself. As in 1286, when the little Maid of Norway inherited the throne, James' heir was a baby girl, Princess Mary. The dying James said despairingly of the Stewart dynasty, 'It cam wi' a lass, it will gang wi' a lass.' He was right, but as it turned out it was not his daughter Mary who was the last Stewart monarch, but Queen Anne, more than a century and a half later.

★

**1543 The Treaty of Greenwich.** Little Queen Mary was betrothed to Prince Edward of England, but Henry VIII's manner was so high-handed that the Scottish Parliament refused to ratify the treaty.

**1544 The Rough Wooing.** This was King Henry's campaign to force the Scots to accept the Treaty of Greenwich and the betrothal of their queen. His orders to his army were to 'put man, woman and childe to fire and sword'. The Lowlands were devastated, but this only made the nation even more determined to resist English dominion.

**1544 The Battle of the Shirts.** John of Moidart, a Macdonald chieftain, defeated a government force at Loch Lochy in a battle that took its name from the hot day on which it was fought. Moidart then retreated to his western fastness and defied the government for another forty years.

**1546 George Wishart Burned at the Stake.** Wishart was an early Protestant preacher, burned for heresy at the orders of David Beaton, Scotland's first cardinal. Beaton, described as 'a bloody butcher' by John Knox, was murdered in revenge by a group of Protestant sympathizers, though it was suspected that Henry VIII might have had a hand in this.

**1547 The Rough Wooing Continued.** Henry VIII died in 1547, but Somerset, the uncle and protector of the young King Edward, continued to fight for his master's Scottish bride. At Pinkie Cleugh near Musselburgh his troops thrashed an army led by the regent, the Earl of Arran, but the Scots refused to come to terms, and Edinburgh Castle continued to hold out.

**1548 The Treaty of Haddington.** Queen Mary, now aged five, was sent to France for safety and was betrothed to the dauphin.

**1549 The Treaty of Veere.** Under this treaty with the Netherlands, Veere became the official port of entry for all Scottish goods, although trade with the Low Countries was long established (in medieval Flanders cod was known as 'aberdaan'). Many Scots later went to study in Holland, since the legal systems were similar, as was the adherence to Calvinist doctrine.

**1550 The Treaty of Boulogne.** After an English army was defeated in France, England agreed to withdraw its troops from Scotland, thus ending the long and painful period of 'rough wooing' and strengthening the Auld Alliance.

**1554 Mary of Guise Became Regent of Scotland.** With the Queen's French mother as head of state, supported by a French army, with Queen Mary herself resident in France and betrothed to the heir to the throne, and government and finance largely controlled by Frenchmen, Scotland looked as if it would become little more than a colony of France.

**1557 The Bond of the Lords of the Congregation.** A group of Protestant nobles, opposed to French rule in Scotland and the marriage of their queen to the dauphin, signed a covenant binding them together against their enemies. This was the signal for attacks on Catholic processions in Edinburgh, when Protestant demonstrators seized the image of St Giles, which they considered to be a popish idol, and ritually 'drowned' it in the Nor' Loch.

**1558 A Royal Marriage.** Queen Mary married the dauphin, Francis. She also signed a secret agreement – which soon leaked out – bequeathing her kingdom to France if she should die before the marriage produced children.

**1558 *The First Blast of the Trumpet against the Monstrous Regiment of Women*** was published, in which John Knox denounced the rule (regiment) of the female Catholics, Mary of Guise in Scotland and Mary Tudor in England.

## John Knox, 1510–72

Knox was a farmer's son from Haddington, educated at St Andrews University. He was ordained a priest and worked as a tutor and notary before being converted to Protestantism by George Wishart. Because of his association in 1546 with the murderers of Cardinal Beaton, Knox was taken prisoner by French forces and served nineteen months as a galley slave. He then took refuge in England, where he was appointed a royal chaplain to the young Protestant King Edward. When the Catholic Queen Mary Tudor succeeded, Knox rapidly left England for Geneva and Frankfurt, where he ministered to the English and Scottish exile congregations and wrote many pamphlets. He preached three times a week – each sermon, it is said, lasting for at least two hours.

Reformist religious ideas had been spreading into Scotland for some time: Lollardy from England in the 1400s and Lutheranism from Germany in the early 1500s made considerable impact, as did the availability of the Bible in English from 1543, but it was when Scottish scholars like Wishart came into contact with Calvinism in Geneva that Protestantism gained a grip in Scotland. After Beaton's death in 1546 there was little active persecution of Protestants, and reformist literature and even anti-Catholic popular songs ('The Paip, that pagan, full o' pride') began to circulate.

In exile, Knox kept in touch with sympathizers in Scotland and returned home in 1559 as the conflict between Mary of Guise and the Lords of the Congregation reached its height. He then played a leading role in the dramatic events of the Reformation (*see* 1559–60). →

When Mary Stuart returned to Scotland as queen, Knox lectured her several times in person and later thundered against her in characteristically abusive sermons. In one he claimed that the Catholic Mass was more dangerous to Scotland than an invasion of 10,000 armed enemies. At the age of fifty he caused a stir by marrying a girl of seventeen, but he was the last man to care what others thought and he continued to serve as minister of St Giles and to preach and write. His *History of the Reformation in Scotland* was a vivid account of the events of 1559–61.

Knox had as good a claim as any man to be the founder of the Scottish Presbyterian Kirk. He was implacably opposed to Catholicism – it was said, 'others snipped at the branches of popery, but he struck at the roots' – and he gave eloquent voice to the beliefs that sustained his fellow Protestants. He was absolutely determined to follow what he believed God had called him to do, and he 'neither feared nor flattered any flesh'. He deliberately targeted his message at the 'commonalty' of Scotland, and advocated the idea that resistance to unlawful or ungodly rulers was fully justified.

# 1559–1560
## THE REFORMATION

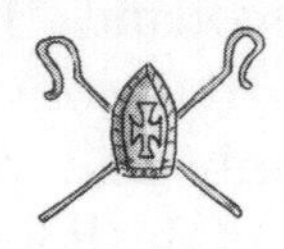

At the beginning of 1559, Scotland was allied to France and was officially a Catholic country under the authority of the Pope in Rome. Those who denied papal authority or preached Protestantism were technically heretics and liable to be burned at the stake. By the end of 1560, the Auld Alliance was over, Scotland was allied to England, had thrown off the authority of the Pope and had created a new national Protestant Church. In dramatic contrast to the previous year, celebrating the Catholic Mass could now result in the death penalty.

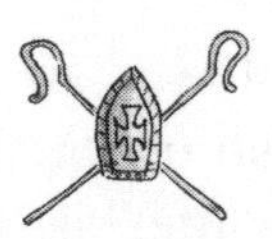

This remarkable turnaround was the outcome of a quick succession of events. John Knox's return to Scotland in 1559 and his inflammatory preaching provoked a series of skirmishes between the royal army and supporters of the Protestant Lords of the Congregation as well as attacks on altarpieces, stained-glass windows and other symbols of Catholic 'superstition'. In early 1560 an English fleet arrived in the Firth of Forth as a result of Queen Elizabeth I's decision to give help to her fellow Protestants in Scotland,

and the Treaty of Berwick was signed to collaborate in expelling the French. This could have been a difficult task, but in June 1560 Mary of Guise died, and the English and French agreed in the Treaty of Edinburgh that they would both withdraw from Scotland. This left the Protestant Lords of the Congregation in control.

Parliament met in July and passed a series of Acts destroying the authority of the Pope, condemning Catholic beliefs and practices and introducing a new Confession of Faith. The organization of the Kirk was dealt with by the *First Book of Discipline*, which outlined a Presbyterian Church in which ministers were to be elected by their congregations and authority would lie with Kirk sessions, overseen by a General Assembly. The *First Book* also covered matters such as the training of ministers, a national system of education and relief for the poor.

The Kirk that emerged was an institution that became inseparable from Scottish national identity and permeated every aspect of Scottish life, since it claimed the right to intervene in both public and private affairs. Critics have said that it produced a society that was narrow and joyless in its outlook, God-fearing rather than God-loving and all too often arrogant, bigoted and hypocritical. But there is no doubt that it also encouraged respect for education, thrift, entrepreneurship and hard work, as well as promoting a healthy questioning of authority.

★

## Mary, Queen of Scots, 1542–87

Brought up at the French court, Mary was eighteen when she returned to Scotland, an educated and accomplished young woman. She was also tall, attractive and vivacious. Her substantial French income meant that she kept a lavish court, lambasted by John Knox for its indulgence in worldly pleasures, and she embarked on a series of progresses around her kingdom, twice travelling north of Inverness.

Her status and personal charms made her a notable catch on the international marriage market, but she refused all offers, including a crafty one by Elizabeth of England, who put forward her own favourite the Earl of Leicester in the belief that she could control Scotland through him. The husband Mary chose in 1565 was Henry Stuart, Lord Darnley, a Catholic with a claim to the thrones of Scotland and England – the marriage thus infuriated Elizabeth. Darnley was a tall, good looking young man, and Mary clearly fancied him greatly. Protestant nobles, shocked by the marriage, started a rebellion that became known as the 'Chaseabout raid', since no real fighting occurred but some of the rebels were chased into exile for a time.

Within a year, Darnley proved to be deeply unsatisfactory as a husband and king consort (as he was styled). He was vain, weak, drunken and almost certainly suffering from syphilis. In 1566 he was involved in the murder, in front of Mary who was six months pregnant, of her Italian servant David Rizzio, of whose closeness to the queen he was jealous. Despite the experience of →

witnessing Rizzio's murder, Mary gave birth to a healthy son, James, who was christened with much splendour at an occasion staged to represent the reconciliation of Protestant and Catholic factions. Darnley sulked and refused to attend.

On the night of 9 February 1567 a violent explosion rocked Kirk o' Field in Edinburgh, where Darnley was staying. He was found strangled in the garden the next morning. James Hepburn, Earl of Bothwell immediately drew suspicion on himself by abducting Mary, and weeks later he divorced his wife and became Mary's third husband. This was too much for the nobility, who confronted the pair at Carberry, near Musselburgh. After tense negotiations, Bothwell was allowed to escape abroad (he died ten years later in chains in a Danish prison) and Mary was imprisoned on Loch Leven, but not before she had endured the attentions of an Edinburgh mob who howled, 'Burn the whore!' at her. She suffered a miscarriage, having been pregnant with twins, and was soon afterwards compelled to abdicate the throne, while her thirteen-month-old son was crowned James VI, with the Earl of Moray as regent.

In 1568 Mary escaped from her island prison on Loch Leven and managed to raise an army, but when they were defeated at the Battle of Langside she crossed the border and threw herself on the mercy of her cousin Elizabeth of England, who promptly put her under house arrest, where she remained for the next nineteen years.

**1561 Queen Mary Returned.** Although briefly Queen of France, when her sickly husband Francis II died, Mary returned to her own kingdom. As well as being Queen of Scots, she also had a claim to the English throne – Catholics who considered Queen Elizabeth to be illegitimate believed Mary was the rightful Queen of England too. Mary was a convinced Catholic, but took advice to 'press no matters of religion' and tolerated Protestants, while privately celebrating Mass in her own household.

**1568–73 Civil War.** Conflict broke out between Queen Mary's supporters and the faction surrounding the young King James. Both sides held parliaments and put out vicious propaganda, and there were many seizures of opponents' goods and land. Two regents were assassinated and a number of prisoners were executed without trial. The turning point came in 1571 when Mary, still a prisoner in England, was suspected of involvement in the Ridolfi plot against Elizabeth. It was now clear that she would not be released to return to Scotland, and when her opponents took Edinburgh Castle in 1573, the war came to an end.

**1569 The Casket Letters.** Letters came to light, allegedly from Mary to Bothwell, which appeared to prove that she had conspired with him to have Darnley murdered. Queen Elizabeth ordered an inquiry into the case but cautiously did not allow it to reach a definite verdict, since she could not allow her cousin and fellow royal to be found guilty of murder. Mary, of course, denied that she had written the letters. The originals have been lost, and most historians believe that they were forgeries put out by Mary's enemies.

**1572 A New Regent.** The Earl of Morton was named regent for the infant King James. The fourth regent since 1567, Morton – who had been one of Rizzio's murderers back in 1566 – was ruthless but competent. He re-established order and confirmed the Protestant religious settlement.

**1577 The Eigg Massacre.** In pursuit of a blood feud started when a party of MacLeods were punished for molesting some MacDonald women, a force of MacLeods killed virtually the entire MacDonald population of the Isle of Eigg, almost 400 people. The MacDonalds had taken refuge in a sea cave and were asphyxiated after the MacLeods lit a fire to smoke them out.

**1581 James VI Came of Age**. A series of palace revolutions culminated in Morton's enemies having the regent condemned to death and executed by the 'Maiden', a sort of early guillotine, which Morton himself had introduced.

**1582 George Buchanan's *History of Scotland*** was published, proposing that the people had the right to depose a tyrannical king.

**1584 The Black Acts.** King James was named head of the Kirk and given the right to appoint bishops and summon the General Assembly. The Acts also barred ministers from preaching on political topics. Strict Presbyterians were outraged. Andrew Melville, their leading spokesman and the man responsible for the *Second Book of Discipline* (1578), which outlined the organization of a Presbyterian Kirk, asserted the doctrine of the 'twa kingdoms': in other words that Church and state were separate and that the king was a subject of the Kirk – he famously called him 'God's silly [weak] vassal'.

**1586 The Treaty of Berwick.** A treaty of mutual defence with England, under which Queen Elizabeth also promised to pay James a pension of £4,000 sterling per annum.

# 1587
## THE EXECUTION OF QUEEN MARY

Technically queen no longer, and imprisoned in various English castles since 1568, James' mother had become a serious embarrassment to the regime of Elizabeth I. As a Catholic with a claim to the English throne she became the focus of Catholic plots to undermine Elizabeth's rule, and in 1582 the English queen asked her gaoler, Sir Amyas Paulet, to contrive an 'accident' to get rid of Mary (he refused). After war with Spain broke out, Mary was found guilty of treason for her involvement in the Babington plot to assassinate Elizabeth – almost certainly a put-up job orchestrated by Elizabeth's spymaster Walsingham – and sentenced to death. Although she hesitated for weeks, Elizabeth finally gritted her teeth and signed her cousin's death warrant.

Mary mounted the scaffold at Fotheringhay Castle in Northamptonshire on 8 February. After forgiving her executioner, she removed her outer clothing to reveal a chemise of deep red, the colour of Catholic martyrdom. It took two strokes of the axe to sever her neck – 'Sweet Jesus', she was heard to murmur after the first blow – and when the executioner lifted her head Mary's auburn wig came away in his hand to reveal grey stubble.

'In my end is my beginning' was the legend embroidered by Mary during her captivity, and her life, loves, captivity

and execution have indeed led to a flood of works of history, psychoanalysis, fantasy and fiction in the centuries since. Her son James, who was already eyeing up his chances of succeeding the childless Elizabeth on the English throne, protested but did nothing – as he said, 'I would not be so fond as to prefer my mother to the title.' He had after all been separated from her at a year old and been brought up to believe that she was the murderess of his father.

⋆

**1589 James Married Anne of Denmark.** He sailed to Oslo for the wedding and was away for six months, suggesting that his control of Scotland was by now secure. The marriage was not a close one but it produced seven children, three of whom survived to adulthood. Anne became a considerable patron of the arts.

**1596 The Rescue of Kinmont Willie.** William Armstrong, known as 'Kinmont Willie', was a Border reiver (cattle rustler) captured by the English authorities and imprisoned in Carlisle. His comrade Walter Scott of Buccleuch ('the Bold Buccleuch') led a daring raid into

England and rescued him the night before his execution. Willie was never recaptured and died in his bed of old age. These events were typical of life in the Borders, a lawless frontier zone where reiving was an accepted practice, along with blood feuds, murder, arson and robbery.

**1600 The Gowrie Conspiracy.** The Earl of Gowrie and his brother were murdered in front of the king. James claimed that the Gowries had been plotting to assassinate him, but there was little proof and the event remains mysterious.

**1600 The Gregorian Calendar Adopted in Scotland.** The year now began officially on 1 January instead of 25 March.

# 1603
## THE UNION OF THE CROWNS

Queen Elizabeth of England died without issue, and her nearest relative was her cousin King James. She had refused to acknowledge him as her successor but James knew that Robert Cecil, the queen's wily chief minister, was preparing the ground for him. When Elizabeth died on 24 March 1603, Robin Carey set off on an epic three-day ride from London to Edinburgh to be the first Englishman to salute his new sovereign.

James wasted little time in heading south, enjoying the cheers of his new subjects who had tired of the rule of the elderly and increasingly tetchy Elizabeth. But the honeymoon was short lived. Accompanying the king were a good many Scots who, like their master, saw the move to richer southern pastures as an opportunity to make their fortune, and they rapidly became notorious for their greed. James wished to make the union of the crowns into a 'perfect union' of England and Scotland, experimenting with designs for a new union flag and styling himself 'King of Great Britain', but was unable to sell the idea to Parliament in either country. Scots were particularly concerned that full union would simply mean the loss of independence and subservience to English rule.

Subjects born after 1603 were considered to hold

a common nationality, the Border region was largely pacified and the exchange rate was fixed at £12 Scots to £1 sterling (although the actual rate varied according to the silver content of coins). James' boast from London was, 'Here I sit and govern Scotland with my pen,' and this he succeeded in doing through able ministers in the north and a new postal service that carried letters from London to Edinburgh in just five days.

★

**1607 The Plantation of Ulster.** Settlers from Scotland were granted land in Ulster that had been confiscated from Catholic rebels. By 1641 more than 20,000 Scots had emigrated there.

**1609 The Statutes of Iona.** Highland clan chiefs were forced to agree to have their eldest sons educated in Lowland schools and taught to read and write English.

## James VI and I, 1566–1625

Separated from his mother and crowned King of Scots when scarcely a year old, James had a difficult childhood. His education at the hands of George Buchanan was harsh but thorough and gave him a lifelong love of intellectual pursuits. He survived the conflicts between various regents who agreed on little other than that the young king be brought up a Protestant.

As a young man he came under the influence of his glamorous French cousin Esme Stuart, whom he created Duke of Lennox, the first in a succession of handsome male 'favourites' to whom he looked for the love he had not received as a child. He also attempted to buy affection through extravagant gifts and hospitality. His redeeming qualities included tolerance in religion, a desire for peace abroad and a keen intelligence.

King James did not always receive a good press from the English: they concentrated on his unprepossessing personal habits such as scratching himself and slobbering at the table, his vanity, his alleged cowardice, his extravagance, his overfondness for handsome young men and the favouritism he showed to his fellow Scots. He was certainly not good at the public relations side of kingship and was happiest when hunting, drinking or discussing poetry and theology with his cronies. When it was suggested to him that he should show himself more to his people, he is said to have replied, 'God's wounds! Shall I pull down my breeks and show them my arse?' But he was an effective and canny ruler, who avoided the traps that led his son Charles I into war with his subjects in both his kingdoms.

**1614 John Napier's *Mirifici Logarithmorum Canonis Descripti*** was published. This consisted of fifty-seven pages of explanation of logarithms accompanied by ninety pages of tables, and became a major aid to the study of physics and astronomy. Known from his birthplace as 'Marvellous Merchiston', Napier was also an astrologer, a magician and the creator of an abacus known as 'Napier's Bones'.

**1616 King James' *Collected Works*** was published, testament to the breadth of James' interests. *Basilikon Doron* and *The Trew Law of Free Monarchies* explored his ideas about government and the divine right of kings ('justly called Gods, for that they exercise a manner of divine power upon earth'); *A Discourse on the Powder Treason* reported on the Gunpowder Plot of 1605; *A Counterblaste to Tobacco* was an attack on smoking ('loathsome to the eye, hateful to the nose, harmful to the brain, dangerous to the lungs'); *Daemonologie* was an investigation of James' long-standing fascination with witchcraft; and there were also poems, speeches and political and theological essays.

**1617 King James Visited Scotland.** When he left for the south in 1603 James assured his Scottish subjects that he would return every two or three years. In fact, this was his only visit and he stayed for just eleven weeks, engaging in fierce disputes with his opponents in the Kirk about whether it should remain independent of royal control.

**1618 The Articles of Perth.** James forced the Kirk to accept a number of unpopular innovations such as kneeling to receive Communion, which smacked of 'popish superstition' to many Scots. The king appeared to have won his battles with the Kirk, imprisoning and then exiling his old adversary Andrew Melville, but his dictatorial line stirred up trouble for the future.

**1620 The Battle of the White Mountain.** This early battle in the Thirty Years' War was a defeat for James' son-in-law, the Elector Frederick of the Palatinate, a German Protestant ruler. The war (1618–48), which pitted Protestants against Catholics and was largely fought in Germany, attracted huge numbers of Scottish mercenary soldiers. It has been estimated that over 40,000 Scots took part in the war, at least half of them in the army of the Protestant champion, Gustavus Adolphus of Sweden. Just one clan, the Munros, provided twenty-seven field officers and eleven captains to the Swedish army.

**1621 The First Scottish Colony.** King James granted a charter for the foundation of the colony of Nova Scotia and subsequently created an order of baronets who in exchange for their title had to provide men or money for the colony. In 1631, however, King Charles I ceded the territory to France.

**1623 Harvest Failures.** There was widespread famine throughout Scotland; some estimates suggest that a quarter of the population of Perth starved to death.

**1625 Charles I Succeeded his Father James to the Throne.** Charles' first act as King of Scots was to claw back all the Church property that landowners had acquired, in some cases as much as 175 years ago. This land grab ('the groundstone of all the mischiefs that followed after') made him intensely unpopular, and he followed it up by appointing bishops to the Privy Council, which alarmed his Presbyterian subjects, and taxing Scotland heavily.

**1633 Charles I's Scottish Coronation.** The king's cold and formal manner did not endear him to his Scottish subjects, who were also distressed by his coronation service. The ritual was conducted in the English manner, and he refused to listen to a petition of ministers, merely ordering them to adopt Anglican practices such as the wearing of vestments, which were seen by the Kirk as 'rags of popery'. When Parliament met, Charles openly noted down the names of those who spoke against his wishes and later had one of them, Lord Balmerino, prosecuted for treason.

**1637 The Prayer Book Riots.** The absentee king and his officious Archbishop of Canterbury, William Laud, ordered the Kirk to accept a new Anglican prayer book. When it was read at a service in St Giles a riot erupted, orchestrated by leading figures in the Kirk, and Jenny Geddes, a market woman, threw her stool at the pulpit crying, 'Will ye say the mass in ma lug?' Then the king's opponents took the first step in what was to become a constitutional revolution: Scotland was declared to be ruled by four 'Tables' consisting of nobles, lairds, burgesses (representatives of the burghs) and ministers.

# 1638

## THE NATIONAL COVENANT

On 28 February a group of nobles led by the Earl of Argyll met at Greyfriars Kirk to sign a document drawn up under the leadership of a minister, Alexander Henderson, and a lawyer, Archibald Johnston of Warriston. The National Covenant – 5,000 words of rather turgid, legalistic prose – rehearsed the so-called Negative Confession of 1581 against Catholicism, listing the religious reforms since 1560. It also denounced King Charles' recent innovations in religion. The signatories bound themselves to defend 'the true religion', and although they also bound themselves to 'support the king' in doing so, the Covenant implied that it was right to resist a king who acted unlawfully and included a demand for 'free' (outside royal control) parliaments and General Assemblies of the Kirk.

When the nobles had signed, copies of the Covenant were sent round the country to be signed by landowners, ministers, the burghs and the general populace. By no means all those eligible to sign did so, but most Scots were now committed to resist the unpopular policies of their absentee monarch.

The Glasgow Assembly of the Kirk followed up the Covenant by declaring bishops to be abolished. King Charles refused to listen to the Covenanters' demands, and so the scene was set for a conflict that would develop into a civil war engulfing all three of Charles' kingdoms – Scotland, England and Ireland – for the next decade and beyond.

★

**1640 The Bishops' Wars.** Relations between the king and the Covenanters soon broke down, and both sides began arming. It was an unequal contest, however; Charles was short of money and mistrusted by many of his English subjects. The scratch army he assembled was ill-trained and reluctant to fight. The Covenanters, by contrast, had no trouble in recruiting experienced soldiers who had served abroad in the Thirty Years' War. Their morale was high, boosted by religious enthusiasm and national pride. The war effort was directed by the Committee of the Three Estates, who, together with the General Assembly of the Kirk, now formed the effective government of Scotland, and the army was led by Alexander Leslie, an experienced general.

The Battle of Newburn on 28 August was brief but decisive. Charles' army was routed and the Covenanters moved on to Newcastle, where they were in a position to throttle London's coal supply, and demanded a payment of £850 per day to maintain their army.

# 1643–1648

## THE CIVIL WAR

In 1642, following the debacle of the Bishops' War, Charles was forced to call his English Parliament. However, relations between King Charles and Parliament broke down and within months civil war erupted in England. The Scots shared many of the political and religious views of Charles' opponents, and under the Solemn League and Covenant of 1643 they agreed to send an army to fight on the Parliamentary side on the understanding that a Presbyterian Church would be established in England.

Thus the Earl of Leven led an army of more than 20,000 men across the border and at Marston Moor near York on 2 July 1644 they linked up with the English Parliamentarians and defeated the Royalists in the largest battle of the civil wars. The king's opponents now had effective control of the north of England, but they gave scant credit to their Scottish allies – a sign of the discord to come.

Some Scots, however, took the king's side, and chief among them was James Graham, Marquis of Montrose. He defeated a much larger Covenanting army at Tippermuir on 1 September 1644 and occupied the city of Perth. This was the start of a civil war within Scotland. Over the next year Montrose won a series of stunning victories across the north, using the Highland charge of his clansmen to devastating effect. But he was unable to stop his Highlanders melting away to secure their booty, and in September 1645 he was defeated at the Battle of Philiphaugh in the Borders and went into exile.

After defeat at the Battle of Naseby (1645) King Charles surrendered to the Scottish army at Newark in 1646. However, they sold their royal prisoner to the English Parliament for £200,000 and retreated back across the border. It soon became clear that the Parliamentarians were not going to establish a Presbyterian Church in England, and many Scots became alarmed by the increasingly radical religious and political beliefs of English victors such as Oliver Cromwell.

In a secret deal with the king known as the Engagement, noble representatives of the Estates promised to invade England in support of a rising by English Royalists. In return, Charles promised, unconvincingly, that he would accept a Presbyterian Church in England and Scotland. The Marquis of Hamilton duly led an army south, but the promised Royalist support did not materialize and he was defeated by Cromwell at the Battle of Preston in August 1648 and subsequently executed.

★

**1648 The Whiggamore Raid.** The Engagement split the Covenanters and the more radical faction, led by the Earl of Argyll, supported a popular uprising with a strong element of social protest in the south-west, known as the Whiggamore Raid (the name, meaning cattle driver, was later shortened to 'Whig' and applied to an English political party from the late 1600s). This led to a period when radical Covenanters held power: they introduced measures to relieve poverty, enacted laws against drunkenness, fornication and witchcraft, abolished lay patronage in the Kirk, and permitted nobles to be prosecuted for adultery.

**1649 The Execution of King Charles I.** The rulers of Scotland made peace with Cromwell, now the leader of the English Parliamentarians. Secure from any threat north of the border, Cromwell then had the king executed at Whitehall in London. This was a step too far for his Scottish subjects. They protested when their king was put on trial in London, but they were not consulted by Cromwell, who proceeded after the king's death to abolish the monarchy and declare in its place a 'commonwealth and free state'. When the news reached Scotland, the instant response was to proclaim Charles' exiled young son as King Charles II of Scots. War was now inevitable.

# 1649–1651

## CIVIL WAR AGAIN

After lengthy negotiations, Charles II agreed reluctantly by the Treaty of Breda (in the Netherlands where he was in exile) to support the Covenant and the establishment of Presbyterianism in Scotland and England. This left the Marquis of Montrose stranded, since Charles had ordered him to raise an army to put pressure on the Covenanters, but now ordered him to disarm. The order failed to reach Montrose, whose army was defeated at Carbisdale in Sutherland in April 1650. Montrose himself was captured and executed in Edinburgh.

The twenty-year-old King Charles landed at the mouth of the Spey in June 1650, which forced Cromwell to act, and he led an army across the border in July. In the ensuing Battle of Dunbar on 3 September, 3,000 Scots were killed and 10,000 taken prisoner. Cromwell himself is said to have laughed uncontrollably at his luck when the Scots' general, David Leslie, abandoned a good position on high ground and left his troops open to a surprise dawn attack. It was no laughing matter for Cromwell's Scottish prisoners, some of whom died on a forced march south, while others were transported as slave labour to North America and the Caribbean.

Defeat at Dunbar almost put paid to Scottish resistance to Cromwell. It also discredited the radical Covenanters, who had insisted on purging the army of all but 'godly' officers, and led to Royalists being recalled into government. On 1 January 1651 Charles II was crowned King of Scots, but was then subjected to a humiliating sermon on the sins of his father and grandfather.

This travesty of a coronation was not forgotten, and Charles never returned to Scotland. In a last desperate fling he led an army south, hoping to recruit Royalist support in England, only to be trounced by Cromwell's larger and better-organized New Model Army at Worcester on 3 September, exactly one year after the Battle of Dunbar. Charles himself escaped into exile, but for Scotland it was the end of the civil wars.

# 1651–1660
## THE COMMONWEALTH

Although the Honours of Scotland (the royal crown, sceptre and sword) were secretly buried under the floor of his kirk by the minister of Kineff in Aberdeenshire, there was no chance of Charles II returning to claim them. Scotland was declared by the London Parliament to be 'one commonwealth with England'; the Scottish Parliament was abolished, and although members from Scotland attended the various London parliaments of the 1650s, some of the 'Scottish' MPs were in fact English army officers. English commissioners were sent north to administer Scotland, and English rule was underpinned by a series of newly built fortresses and the presence of an army of 10,000 men under General Monck.

The attitude of the English to their new partners was generally condescending and was summed up by a minister who described Scotland's part in the union as 'when a poor bird is embodied into the hawk that hath eaten it up'. However, the regime did restore and preserve law and order. Free trade with England benefited some Scottish merchants, and economic prosperity revived. The universities flourished, as did cultural and intellectual life. In practice, most Scots came to accept the regime.

In the vexed question of religion the Republic practised some tolerance. Bishops were abolished and Catholicism was outlawed, but all Protestant denominations were allowed. This distressed many Presbyterians who wished the Kirk to be the sole church and the General Assembly – which was dissolved – to be its ruling body. The Kirk itself was split between the royalist Resolutioners and the more radical Protesters, and, though Cromwell hoped they would resolve their differences, the division remained.

★

**1653 Rabelais Translated.** Sir Thomas Urquhart, a Royalist laird from Cromarty, was an extravagant and eccentric figure who wrote on many subjects. His translation of Rabelais' bawdy tales became a classic, often described as 'more Rabelaisian than Rabelais himself'. He is said to have died laughing at the news of Charles II's restoration.

**1654 Blaeu's *Novus Atlas*** published, containing forty-seven regional maps, making Scotland one of the best-mapped countries in Europe.

**1660 The Restoration.** After Oliver Cromwell's death in 1658 the Republic in England collapsed into anarchy. In response, conservative English parliamentarians asked General Monck, the commander-in-chief of the army in

Scotland, to bring his disciplined troops south to restore order. Monck recalled the pre-civil war Parliament, who promptly invited Charles II to return from exile. Scots rejoiced at the restoration of their king and what they thought would be the end of English rule and exorbitant taxation. A day of public thanksgiving was declared, and there were celebrations in the streets of Edinburgh, including a firework display representing Cromwell being hounded by the devil.

However, the new king's treatment of Scotland did not echo the Scots' appreciation. Charles appointed officials and counsellors with no reference to Parliament, had a number of his enemies executed, passed a series of Acts giving virtually absolute power to the crown and repealed all Acts passed since 1633. Thus bishops were reimposed on the Kirk, and the National Covenant was declared illegal.

**1664 The Conventicles Act.** Ministers who refused to accept Charles II's religious settlement were forcibly excluded from their parishes and started to hold informal services or 'conventicles', often in the open air and sometimes attended by thousands of worshippers. The Conventicles Act was an attempt to stamp out this practice, and preaching at a conventicle ultimately became punishable by death.

**1666 The Pentland Rising.** An army of Covenanters from Galloway who marched on Edinburgh, outraged by the persecution of conventicles, was defeated at Rullion Green. The Covenanters, men of humble birth, were treated with great savagery: a number were tortured, other were executed or transported to the West Indies.

**1670 The Edinburgh Botanic Garden** was founded at Holyrood Park.

**1672 The High Court of Justiciary** was established as the supreme criminal court of Scotland.

**1678 The Highland Host.** An army of Highlanders, many of them Catholics, was let loose on the south-west to enforce obedience to the religious laws and punish Covenanters. The rapacious behaviour of the Highlanders brought open rebellion by the Covenanters closer.

**1679 The Murder of Archbishop Sharp.** A hate figure for Covenanters, the former Presbyterian minister Sharp was now the symbol of royal rule over the Kirk. His murder by a group of desperate Covenanters, who dragged him from his coach and killed him in front of his daughter, was the signal for a wider uprising. An armed conventicle at Drumclog beat off the attack of Graham of Claverhouse ('Bluidy Clavers'), but the Covenanters were defeated at Bothwell Brig by the Duke of Monmouth, King Charles' illegitimate son. Savage reprisals followed against the Covenanters.

**1680 The First Free Public Lending Library in Scotland** was founded at Innerpeffray near Crieff by David Drummond, Lord Madertie.

# 1680–1688

## THE KILLING TIME

On 22 June 1680 Richard Cameron, a conventicle preacher, read a declaration in the square of Sanquhar in Dumfries renouncing allegiance to Charles II and his government in Scotland, and claiming that the king had 'tyrannized' on the throne. In response, Charles appointed his Catholic brother James, Duke of York, as Commissioner in Scotland and started a campaign against the Covenanters that acquired the grim name of the 'Killing Time'.

The only pitched battle was at Airds Moss in Kyle, where Cameron himself was killed, but his followers, known as Cameronians, retaliated by announcing the excommunication of the king, his brother and other

Royalist leaders. Hunted by the dragoons of Sir George Mackenzie ('Bluidy Mackenzie'), the Covenanters took to the hills. They continued to hold to the belief that there was 'nae king but Christ' and to hold conventicles in secret. When caught or informed on they were killed out of hand by the dragoons or subjected to appalling punishments. Two women were tied to stakes in Wigtown Bay and left to be drowned by the incoming tide. One unfortunate was sentenced as follows: 'His right hand to be struck off, and after some time his left. That he is to be hanged up and cut down alive, his bowels to be taken out and his heart shown by the hangman to the people.'

★

**1681 Stair's *Institutions of the Law of Scotland* Published**. This great work, based on the principles of Roman law with Dutch and French commentaries, systematized the whole of Scots law and is still cited in court today.

**1682 The Advocates Library Founded**, later becoming the National Library of Scotland.

**1683 John Reid's *The Scots Gard'ner* Published**. This manual of horticulture made the first mention of the cultivation of potatoes in Scotland.

**1685 The Death of Charles II.** Catholic King James VII, who succeeded his brother, confirmed that anyone signing the Covenant was guilty of treason and ordered that attendance at a conventicle should be punishable by death.

**1688 The Glorious Revolution.** The Dutch Protestant ruler, William of Orange, husband of James' daughter Mary, invaded England and replaced King James. The news was greeted with joy in Scotland. Ex-King James' officials were driven out, the Catholic chapel at Holyrood was desecrated and ministers who acknowledged the authority of bishops were ejected.

**1689 The Claim of Right.** A parliament was summoned and after acrimonious debate finally agreed to offer the Scottish crown to William and Mary jointly, as had been decided in England. Parliament's declaration, the Claim of Right, was a more radical document than its English equivalent, the Bill of Rights. Unlike the English version, it made clear that King James had not abdicated but been deposed, and demanded religious and political freedoms.

**1689 The Battle of Killiecrankie.** William and Mary were not universally supported in Scotland. Jacobites, the supporters of King James, still had a strong presence, especially in the Highlands, and it was here that Graham of Claverhouse (Viscount Dundee) raised an army. He led them to a stunning victory at Killiecrankie in Perthshire, but 'Bonny Dundee' was killed in the battle, and his forces scattered.

# 1692
# THE MASSACRE OF GLENCOE

On the night of 13 February, thirty-eight MacDonalds of Glencoe, including their chief Alasdair MacIain and a number of women and children, were murdered by government troops led by Captain Robert Campbell of Glenlyon. This was not a clan feud (most of the soldiers were not Campbells), but rather the deliberate attempt by government to stamp out Jacobite support in the Highlands.

It was decided to make an example of the MacDonalds of Glencoe. King William signed an order to 'extirpate' Highland rebels, and 'letters of fire and sword' were issued against the MacDonalds by Sir John Dalrymple, the Lord Advocate. The original plan was to seal off Glencoe with hundreds of soldiers and conduct what would now be called ethnic cleansing of the area. This did not happen, but the outcome was terrible enough. After enjoying the hospitality of the MacDonalds for some weeks, Captain Robert Campbell received orders to turn on his hosts and 'put to the sword all under seventy', especially not allowing 'the old fox' (MacIain) and his sons to escape. MacIain was murdered in his bed, and though a good many MacDonalds did escape into the hills, the soldiers torched their houses, and many died of exposure.

An official inquiry into the massacre put the blame on Dalrymple, but he escaped serious punishment and had

returned to government by 1700. From the government's point of view the massacre was completely counter-productive, since it only stimulated Jacobite feeling in the Highlands.

★

**1693–1700 The Lean Years.** A series of harvest failures led to terrible famines. Some estimates put the death toll in the 1690s at over ten per cent of the population. Tens of thousands of Scots emigrated to Ireland.

**1695 The Bank of Scotland** was established by Act of Parliament. Unlike the Bank of England (1694) it was not connected with government but set up to support business.

**1696 The Act for Settling of Schools** was passed, requiring every parish to establish a school and employ a schoolmaster.

**1697 The Execution of Thomas Aikenhead.** A young theology student from Edinburgh, Aikenhead was overheard ridiculing Christianity. His execution for blasphemy was almost the last manifestation of the bigoted spirit in the Kirk that interpreted Scotland's troubles in the seventeenth century as a punishment for sin, and took it out on those who were different: homosexuals sentenced to be strangled, alleged witches burned at the stake, the Catholic Irish followers of Montrose butchered in cold blood after the Battle of Philiphaugh (1645) or the Highlanders so casually murdered at Glencoe.

# 1698
# THE DARIEN SCHEME

In July five ships sailed from Leith for Central America with the aim of establishing a Scottish colony, New Caledonia, on the isthmus of Panama, known then as Darien. The scheme was the brainchild of William Paterson, a London-based Scottish businessman. The idea was reasonable: to establish a colony that could carry goods across the narrow isthmus, near where the Panama Canal now is, between the Caribbean and Pacific, cutting out the long and dangerous sea voyage round Cape Horn. But the expedition itself was a disaster.

The project attracted enormous interest and investment. More than £300,000 was raised, a substantial fraction of Scotland's available capital; among the investors were small businessmen as well as big landowners and the rich. But from the start things went wrong. English investors pulled out under pressure from the East India Company, who saw the venture as unwelcome competition. The expedition itself was incompetently led and poorly supplied – Bibles and woollen hats were never going to be successful trade goods in Central America. On landing, the colonists founded the settlements of New Edinburgh and Fort St Andrew, but fever, uncooperative natives, quarrels among the leadership and opposition from Spain all presented insuperable problems.

A second expedition sailed in 1699, but this had no better success, and in 1700 the surviving colonists surrendered to Spain. In all some 2,000 lives were lost, and Scotland was virtually bankrupted.

★

**1701 The Act of Settlement.** The English Parliament laid down that if King William's heir, his sister-in-law Anne, died without issue, the throne should pass to the Electress Sophia of Hanover, the Protestant granddaughter of James VI, and her heirs. The Act was aimed at preventing the return of the Stuarts in the form of James, also known as the 'Old Pretender', son of the exiled James VII. The Scottish Parliament were not consulted in the matter, however, and therefore were not obliged to accept the Act. Indeed, many Englishmen thought that James would be offered the throne of Scotland; consequently moves began towards uniting the two countries in order to prevent this happening.

**1702 The Death of King William.** Dutch William was unpopular in Scotland, and not just with Jacobites, who toasted James, their 'king over the water', and later 'the little gentleman in black velvet', the mole over whose hill King William's horse stumbled and threw him to his death. Even more of a foreigner than his two predecessors, and with no Stuart blood in his veins, William governed Scotland through London-based ministers and engaged in an unpopular war with France that cost Scotland dearly in taxation and lost trade. Queen Anne, who took the throne after William's death, had little knowledge or love of Scotland, and her government continued to follow similar policies, including the ultimate aim of uniting her kingdoms.

**1703 Martin Martin's *Description of the Western Isles of Scotland* Published**. This provided an insight into a world whose culture remained completely distinct from the rest of Scotland.

# 1707
# THE ACT OF UNION

On 16 January Parliament ratified by 110 votes to 69 the Treaty of Union that created a new state, the 'United Kingdom of Great Britain', and transferred parliamentary sovereignty to a new body formed from the united Parliaments of England and Scotland. Scotland was to keep its own legal system and established Presbyterian Church, but its status as an independent nation was at an end. As Chancellor Seafield put it, 'Now there's ane end to ane auld song.'

Nothing in Scottish history is more controversial than the Union. Nationalists say that Scots were betrayed by their leaders, who were 'bought and sold for English gold'. Unionists point to the economic, political and military weakness of Scotland and the desirability of union with its stronger and richer neighbour. Certainly a substantial sum of money was distributed among the Scottish nobility, but it is equally true that half of Scotland's foreign trade was across the border and the failure of the Darien Scheme had left the economy in a desperate state.

The Union itself was the result of short-term political factors. The union of the crowns was no longer sustainable when the parliaments of England and Scotland were at loggerheads as they had been, passing tit-for-tat Acts concerning the succession to the throne, ever since 1701. And if the alternative to union was a Jacobite (and Catholic) succession, then many Scots preferred union. After all, it was by no means certain that it would be permanent.

When the Union was announced, it was greeted with howls of protest. In its last months Parliament received a flood of petitions against the proposal, and there were riots in many towns, so severe that martial law was declared. A contemporary observer declared that the Union was 'contrary to the inclinations of at least three fourths of the Kingdom'. The bells of St Giles were rung to the tune of 'Why am I so Sad on my Wedding Day'. But all protest was ignored by Scotland's ruling class, Burns' 'parcel of rogues'.

Once in place, the Union delivered increased security to England, but did little for Scotland. The new British Parliament was in practice just the English Parliament with the addition of a few Scottish members (only 16 Scottish Lords against the 190 English, and 45 Scottish

MPs against 513 English). In the short term, even the economic advantages of union did not materialize. And for this, Scotland had surrendered its independence, even if it preserved some of its distinctive institutions. Unionist historians point to the positive impact of the Union in the long term, delivering opportunities for Scottish business and for individual Scots through the Industrial Revolution and participation in the British Empire. But nationalists maintain that an independent Scotland could have prospered equally, while developing along its own path.

★

**1708 The Old Pretender.** James Stuart sailed into the Firth of Forth and attempted to land a force of 6,000 men, but was beaten back by bad weather and the Royal Navy. There was considerable panic in London, and a number of Scottish nobles were arrested.

**1709 The Scottish Society for Promoting Christian Knowledge (SSPCK) Founded.** It had the express mission in the Highlands of eradicating 'popery' and the Gaelic language.

**1710 A Public Ball in Edinburgh.** This was a sign that the 'moderate' party were now in control of the Kirk, yet it was some decades before they could bring themselves to allow a public theatrical performance.

**1712 The Patronage Act.** The Act restored to landowners the right to appoint parish ministers. This outraged many Scots, and was seen as typical of the patronizing attitude of the English, who believed that Scotland was merely a

# Rob Roy, 1671–1734

The MacGregors had long been known as troublemakers – a royal order of the early seventeenth century referred to them as 'a wicked and rebellious race' and their name itself was banned. Robert MacGregor, later known as Rob Roy (*ruadh* meaning 'red', from his red hair), was no exception. At the age of eighteen he joined his father in Bonny Dundee's Jacobite army at the Battle of Killiecrankie (*see* 1689) and for much of the rest of his life he was a thorn in the side of authority.

Rob Roy was a cattleman. This meant many things: he owned cattle, he dealt in them, he drove them south to more profitable markets. But he was also involved in the shadier side of the business. Cattle 'lifting' or rustling was widespread, and the armed men Rob Roy employed to protect his own beasts sometimes turned to raiding the cattle of their clan enemies or demanding protection money, known as 'black meal'. →

In 1712 Rob Roy defaulted on a loan from the Duke of Montrose. He was branded an outlaw, his lands were seized and his wife and family evicted. He fled to the hills and for the next decade engaged in open war against the duke and his allies. This included joining the Jacobite cause during the Fifteen and at the Battle of Glenshiel in 1719 and raiding the property of the duke and his allies, which he sometimes redistributed among the poor, thus earning himself the image of a Scottish Robin Hood. Several dramatic escapes from captivity and a series of duels, in which his broad shoulders and abnormally long arms stood him in good stead, added to his reputation.

The story of Rob Roy lived on in literature. Daniel Defoe's *Highland Rogue* (1723) made him famous in his own lifetime and Walter Scott's novel (1817) elaborated the legend further. A successful film in 1995 was more accurate than most of cinema's excursions into Scottish history.

junior partner in the Union and they could do with it what they wished.

**1713 Scrapping the Union.** Lord Seafield introduced a motion in the House of Lords to repeal the Act of Union. Every single Scottish peer supported the motion, and it was only narrowly defeated.

**1715 The Fifteen.** Queen Anne, the last Stuart monarch, died in 1714, and was succeeded by the Hanoverian George I. This was the signal for a Jacobite rising, and the Earl of Mar, known as 'Bobbing John' for his change of sides, raised the Stuart royal standard at Braemar in the name of 'King James VIII' (the Old Pretender, also known as 'the Chevalier'). The promised help from France did not materialize, however, and Mar fatally delayed, allowing loyalist support to gather. The Battle of Sheriffmuir, near Dunblane, was a draw, despite the Jacobites' superior numbers; the momentum of the rising was gone. The Chevalier himself arrived a month after Sheriffmuir, but his gloomy and unattractive personality did nothing for the cause. By early 1716 the rising had collapsed, and he sailed from Montrose back to France, never to return.

**1719 The Battle of Glenshiel**. In the final Jacobite rising before 1745, a small Spanish force landed in the north-west. They attracted little support and were easily defeated in a skirmish.

**1722 Rob Roy MacGregor** surrendered to the Duke of Montrose.

**1723 The Honourable Society of Improvers Founded** in Edinburgh. The first of many such societies, its landowning members aimed at encouraging improvements in agriculture. In place of the antiquated and wasteful systems of runrig (strip farming) and infield/outfield cultivation, they promoted enclosure of the old open fields, 'scientific' methods such as crop rotation, new crops such as the potato, and selective breeding to produce bigger and better animals.

**1724 General George Wade** began the construction of 250 miles of new roads and forty new bridges in the western and central Highlands.

**1725 The Malt Tax** introduced by London, hitting the brewing and distilling trades, raised the price of drink and caused serious and widespread riots. Order was restored by the Lord Justice General, Archibald Campbell, Earl of Islay and later Duke of Argyll. For most of the next thirty-five years he dominated Scottish politics as the 'uncrowned king of Scotland' – although, like many Scottish aristocrats from this time on, he was actually born and educated in England, where he spent much of his life.

**1726 Allan Ramsay**, a wig maker, poet and editor, opened a bookshop and lending library in Edinburgh.

**1726 The Medical Faculty of the University of Edinburgh** was founded; within fifty years it became the leading medical school in Britain.

**1727 The Burning of Janet Horne**, at Dornoch in a barrel of tar, having been found guilty of witchcraft, was the last such execution in Scotland.

**1736 The Porteous Riots.** 'Black Jock' Porteous, the captain of the Edinburgh town guard, was lynched by a mob who objected to his harsh treatment of smugglers. At this time, because of heavy taxes imposed by London, smuggling was a major source of income for many Scots.

**1739 David Hume's *Treatise of Human Nature* Published.** One of the most influential works of philosophy ever published, this was the founding text of the intellectual movement that became known as the Scottish Enlightenment.

## David Hume, 1711–76

Hume is widely recognized as the most important philosopher ever to write in English. The son of a Berwickshire landowning family, he was intellectually precocious – his mother described him as 'uncommonly wake-minded' – and he went up to Edinburgh University at the age of twelve. But he never graduated and then tried his hand unsuccessfully at a variety of jobs in law and business, suffering depression that came close to nervous breakdown, before he fixed on a career as a writer.

During three years of reading and study in France he drafted his *Treatise of Human Nature*, which was a systematic inquiry into human intellect, emotions and morality. The book was infused with Hume's sceptical, rational approach and his rejection of religious dogma. Its initial reception disappointed him – 'It fell dead-born from the press,' he said – but he continued to produce political and philosophical essays while holding jobs as a tutor and private secretary. Because he was known to be an atheist who described the idea of life after death as 'a most unreasonable fancy', he was refused professorships at Edinburgh and Glasgow and never held any academic post.

The work that made his name and fortune was his six-volume *History of England*, published from 1754, over a million words long and the standard work on the subject for many years. His reputation established, Hume enjoyed a period in Paris where he was feted by French intellectuals and entertained by society ladies. On his return to Edinburgh he formed a liaison with Nancy Orde, thirty years his junior. The →

high-spirited young woman chalked 'St David's Street' on the wall of the great man's house, and the street still bears this name.

Hume's work was immensely influential on his contemporaries and successors. His friend Adam Smith applied Hume's empirical ideas to his study of economics. Immanuel Kant said that 'Hume woke me from my dogmatic slumbers.' Figures as diverse as the utilitarian philosopher Jeremy Bentham and Charles Darwin, the father of evolution, acknowledged Hume's influence.

**1740 The Black Watch Founded** – the first of many Highland regiments in the British army, originally charged with policing the Highlands.

**1740 'Rule Britannia'** written by James Thomson, who was born and educated in Scotland, although he spent most of his working life in England.

**1743 The Last Wolf in Scotland Killed** on the Findhorn River in Moray by a hunter named McQueen.

**1744 The Honourable Company of Edinburgh Golfers Founded**, the world's first golf club.

# 1745

## THE FORTY-FIVE

On 23 July Charles Edward Stuart, 'Bonny Prince Charlie', the son of the Old Pretender, landed on Eriskay in the Outer Hebrides. King Louis XV of France had promised to provide the prince with an army, but when the French pulled out he went ahead anyway, accompanied by just seven followers ('the seven men of Moidart'). On 19 August the royal standard was raised at Glenfinnan, near Fort William, by which time the clans had started to rally to the Jacobite cause. When Donald Cameron of Lochiel came out, declaring, 'I'll share the fate of my Prince,' support started to snowball, and the Jacobite army soon took Perth.

Edinburgh was next, where Charles held court at Holyrood and proclaimed his father as 'King James VIII'. On 21 September a surprise attack routed the government troops of Sir John Cope at the Battle of Prestonpans, a few miles east of Edinburgh – Jacobites celebrated the victory by singing the ballad 'Hey Johnnie Cope, Are ye Waking Yet?'. By now there was considerable alarm in London: troops were summoned back from the Continent and a morale-boosting new verse about crushing rebellious Scots was added to 'God Save the King'.

The question for the prince was what to do next. A council of war decided by a majority of just one to march south – Lord George Murray, the Jacobites' brilliant general, voted against – and on 3 November an army of some 6,000 men set off. They made phenomenal progress, reaching Derby, just 120 miles from London, in a month. But they did not recruit support in England as they had hoped, government forces were approaching and there was word of disaffection back in Scotland. One of the great 'what-ifs' of history is what would have happened if they had pressed on to London, where their success had caused panic. But in the event, only the prince himself was in favour of continuing to advance and he was forced, rather sulkily, to give in to his advisers. On 6 December, the army started to march back north.

# 1746

## THE BATTLE OF CULLODEN

Back in Scotland, the Jacobites defeated a government army at the Battle of Falkirk on 17 January but were then forced to retreat north. They reached Inverness short of supplies and with an army reduced by desertions to about 5,000 men. Charles rejected the sound advice of Lord George Murray to wage a guerrilla campaign against the Duke of Cumberland's pursuing troops and insisted on confronting the larger Hanoverian army in battle. The site he chose was a bare, flat piece of moorland, eminently suited to the Hanoverians' strengths in artillery and cavalry, but much less appropriate for mounting the traditional downhill charge of his Highland infantry. On 16 April the last pitched battle on British soil was joined, and it was all over in less than an hour. Cumberland's artillery cut the Jacobite ranks to pieces, and when they charged they were mown down by a withering crossfire from his disciplined infantry.

The prince, seeing that the day was lost, gave the order that every man should save himself and fled from the field. A thousand Jacobites were killed in the battle, but it was afterwards that Cumberland, just twenty-four years old, earned his nickname 'Butcher'. His orders were to 'harry, burn and kill men, women and children'. The wounded were slaughtered and their bodies mutilated, and fugitives from the battle were hunted down and killed along with their families in an almost genocidal campaign of terror. Leading Jacobites were arrested, many forfeited their lands and some were executed, including Lord Lovat, the last man to be beheaded in Britain, at Tower Hill in London.

No episodes in Scottish history have been more distorted by myth, romance and nostalgia than the Forty-Five and Culloden. This was not a war between Scotland and England, or even a war between Lowlands and Highlands. Many Highland clans supported the Hanoverians, and Cumberland's army at Culloden contained more Scots than Prince Charlie's did. In some ways it was a civil war within Scotland, but what was at stake was the throne of the United Kingdom. Many Jacobites supported the prince out of patriotism, because he represented Scotland's ancestral ruling dynasty. It all made for a romantic story, but it was also a dead end. Defeat at Culloden killed off the Jacobite cause, which probably never stood a chance anyway because a majority of Scots, let alone the English, would not support a Catholic ruler, and the promised French aid did not appear.

The government took good care that the Highlands would not rise again: a Disarming Act (1747) removed the clans' weapons and banned Highland dress and bagpipe music, forts and garrisons were placed at strategic points, and Highlanders – even from Jacobite clans – were recruited into the British army. The greatest impact of the Forty-Five was on the Highlanders themselves. Clan chiefs now demanded rent from their tenants instead of service in battle, emigration increased, the region was opened up to the outside world and its distinctive culture began to fade.

★

## Prince Charlie, 1720–88

Prince Charlie was born and educated in Rome and spent all his early life in Italy and France. Until he landed on Eriskay in 1745 he had never seen Scotland, and his opponents capitalized on his foreignness by calling him a 'popish Italian'.

However, the prince had a number of things in his favour: he had already gained military experience in the French army; he was prepared to gamble, as in his decision to go ahead without French support and later to lead his army across the border into England; most importantly, he had the glamour, energy and charisma that his dour father so patently lacked and he understood how to win the clansmen over. When, soon after his landing, MacDonald of Boisdale urged him to go home, Charlie disarmed him completely by replying, 'I am come home.'

He can be blamed for some bad decisions in the course of 1745 and 1746 – lingering in Edinburgh rather than hurrying to London, and insisting on giving pitched battle at Culloden – but it was after the final defeat that his finest hour arrived. He left the battlefield of Culloden in tears ('there you go for a damned cowardly Italian' was the unkind comment of the colonel of his Lifeguards) and spent the next five months as a fugitive in the Highlands and Islands. Sometimes he had just two or three companions, and in the face of the constant dangers and hardships of life on the run his unfailing courage and cheerfulness won the hearts of all who met him. Despite the price of £30,000 on his head none of his people betrayed him, and he finally reached France after leaving Skye disguised as →

'Betty Burke', the maid of Flora MacDonald.

Prince Charlie returned to Italy and wandered the Continent for another four decades, visiting London in secret several times, declaring he would convert to Protestantism and styling himself 'King Charles III of Great Britain' after his father died. But he wasted his last chance of restoration in 1759 when he turned up drunk at a meeting to discuss a possible French invasion of England; he increasingly consoled himself with alcohol and love affairs. He married briefly but had no legitimate children, and when his brother Henry died in 1807 the Stuart line came to an end.

**1747 The British Linen Company**. Based in Edinburgh, the company started to give loans to linen manufacturers, greatly stimulating the trade. Scotland now began to see some economic benefits from the Union, and industries such as linen, wool, fisheries and mining began to grow.

**1748 Robert Adam** joined the family architecture practice in Edinburgh and went on to design many of the greatest neoclassical buildings in England and Scotland, including Register House and Charlotte Square in Edinburgh.

**1755 Reverend Alexander Webster's Census.** This privately conducted census, the first of its kind, recorded the population of Scotland at 1,265,380, approximately a fifth that of England.

**1758 The Tobacco Lords.** Scotland's imports of tobacco from America overtook England's. The Atlantic trade led to the rapid growth of Glasgow and the emergence of the 'tobacco lords', fabulously wealthy merchants who made their fortune from the weed and built themselves magnificent villas in the west of the city.

**1759 The Battle of Quebec.** Prime Minister William Pitt sent two Highland regiments to Canada to fight the French in the Seven Years' War, since, he reasoned, they were cheaper than using German mercenaries and more expendable too. 'Not many will return,' he casually remarked when dispatching them overseas. In fact, they played an important part in defeating the French at Quebec, after General Wolfe, who had fought at Culloden, placed them in the front line since, he said, it would be 'no great mischief if they fall'. In the next fifty years a dozen regiments of kilted Highlanders were raised and became an integral part of the British army.

**1760 The Carron Ironworks.** Located on the banks of the river Carron, near Falkirk, the works used the new technique of coke-fired smelting. Their fortune was assured when they started to produce a new sort of cannon for the

Royal Navy – short-barrelled, quickly reloadable guns, which became known as 'carronades'. By 1814 Carron was the largest ironworks in Europe and by 1850 Scotland was producing a quarter of Britain's iron.

**1760 Joseph MacDonald's *Compleat Theory*** was published, the first study of the Highland bagpipe and its music.

**1762 The First Scottish Prime Minister.** The Earl of Bute was an unpopular figure and only held the position briefly. This was a time when Scots generally were unpopular in the England – in a notorious incident two Highland officers were pelted with apples at the theatre in Covent Garden amid cries of 'No Scots! Out with them!' – but this was a result of the English finally waking up to the fact that Scotland was a full partner in the Union and many Scots were doing very well out of it.

**1763 'The Noblest Prospect Which a Scotchman Ever Sees**, is the high road that leads him to England,' was one of Dr Johnson's many Scottophobic remarks, recorded

## James Boswell, 1740–95

'I do indeed come from Scotland,' said Boswell, 'but I cannot help it.'

'That, sir, I find', replied Dr Johnson, 'is what a very great number of your countrymen cannot help.'

These were the first words exchanged by the great doctor, aged fifty-three and at the height of his literary powers, and Boswell, a young law student of twenty-two with a taste for celebrities and an appetite for debauchery. They hit it off instantly, became regular companions, and after Johnson's death in 1791 Boswell published his masterpiece, *The Life of Samuel Johnson.* It was a revolutionary sort of biography, not just a dry record of his hero's career but a fully rounded portrait, complete with direct speech and many personal and human details.

Boswell's father, a judge, had sent him to Glasgow University at nineteen but he soon ran away to London and later travelled on the Continent. As well as producing a good deal of journalism, he finally qualified as a lawyer in Edinburgh and later in London, but had little success in the profession. Much of his life was a tension between, on one hand, the need to earn a living and on the other, →

the desire for literary fame, the company of great men and the temptation of worldly pleasures.

His keen powers of observation were evident in the diary that he kept for long periods from the age of eighteen, and which was only rediscovered in the 1920s. In it he subjected his life and emotions to pitiless examination, frankly reporting on his mood swings, his drinking and gambling and his extremely active sex life. He married a wife who tolerated his irregularities, but when she died, leaving him with six children, his drinking and the gonorrhoea he had caught as a young man in London got the better of him.

by his friend and biographer, James Boswell. In fact, there was some truth in it, despite Scotland's growing prosperity and intellectual renown. In the same year a crowded meeting of Edinburgh's Select Society heard an address by an actor on how to eliminate Scotticisms from their speech, in case they should appear provincial in London society.

**1765 James Watt Developed the Separate Condenser**, the most important of the many improvements he made to the steam engine, the driving force of the Industrial Revolution. Watt was a mathematical instrument maker from Greenock, and the original idea of the condenser came to him as he walked on Glasgow Green.

**1765 The Ossian Forgeries.** James Macpherson published his 'translations' of ancient Gaelic poems supposedly composed by the bard Ossian. They became immensely popular and sold in huge numbers throughout Europe (Napoleon was a great fan). Macpherson jumped successfully on the

## The Scottish Enlightenment

David Hume announced in 1757 that the Scots were 'the people the most distinguished for Literature in Europe'. This may have been a patriotic boast, but others agreed with him at the time. Voltaire, the celebrated French writer and philosopher, declared that, 'It is to Edinburgh that we must look for our intellectual tastes and our idea of civilization.' An English visitor remarked, 'Here I stand at what is called the Cross of Edinburgh, and can, in a few minutes, take fifty men of genius and learning by the hand.'

The second half of the eighteenth century saw an extraordinary explosion of intellectual activity in Scotland. Literary clubs and scientific and debating societies flourished, as did publishers and booksellers. Newspapers and journals multiplied. The universities – at a time when Oxford and Cambridge were sunk in sloth – were staffed by men with European reputations. Scots such as Hume, Kames and Robertson wrote a new sort of analytical history. Other scholars effectively invented the social sciences we now call sociology, anthropology and economics, and applied systematic methods to the study of other subjects, including law and linguistics. The physical sciences, too, saw remarkable advances by men such as James Hutton, the father of modern geology. Edinburgh became known as the 'Athens of the North', but the Enlightenment was also a feature of Aberdeen – where the characteristic school of 'common sense' philosophy developed – and Glasgow, where Adam Smith wrote his groundbreaking works on economics.

All of this activity was 'enlightened' because →

bandwagon of Romantic fascination with a misty distant past; but even at the time some critics believed that he made the whole thing up, as he certainly did.

**1766 Edinburgh's New Town**. The architect James Craig, just twenty-two, was quite unknown, but the rectangular grid of streets that he devised not only gentrified 'Auld Reekie' but developed the area into one of the most elegant residential quarters in any European city.

its practitioners rejected superstition, religious dogma and established authorities, and subjected their fields of study to rational, sceptical, scientific scrutiny. This was not a new approach – the Enlightenment began in France – but Scots were particularly tenacious in their questioning and often gave their studies a more practical slant. It is not surprising that medicine, law, engineering and finance became and remain especially strong disciplines in Scotland.

Why did all this happen? Partly it was because the 'moderates' came to the fore in the Kirk, men who were less bigoted in their views and prepared to tolerate enquiry in science and philosophy. But more importantly it was because Scotland was by European standards a notably educated and literate country. Schooling was far in advance of England, including at university level – there were more university places, they were cheaper and a university education was thus accessible to Scots from even quite humble homes. The thrifty, clever, hard-working 'lad o'pairts', arriving at university with his sack of oatmeal as rations for the term, became a classic embodiment of Scottish values.

**1768** ***Encyclopaedia Britannica*** was first published in Edinburgh, confidently declaring that it 'digested the different Arts and Sciences into distinct Treatises or Systems'.

**1769 Thomas Pennant's *Tour of Scotland* Published.** This was a popular read for those who wished to learn about 'North Britain' and a valuable record of Scotland's natural history and antiquities.

**1771 The First Knitting Machines** were used in Hawick, marking the start of a rapid expansion of the textile industry in the Borders.

**1773 A Tour of the Highlands.** James Boswell persuaded Dr Johnson to accompany him on a trip to the Highlands. On Skye they saw a dance performed 'which the emigration from Skye has occasioned'. When Boswell asked the name of the dance, he was told, 'America'. It was a sign of the times, since emigration from the Highlands was soon to increase enormously.

**1776 Adam Smith's *Wealth of Nations* Published**, the most influential book ever written on economics.

**1777 No Slavery.** In the case of Joseph Knight, an African brought to Scotland as a slave, the Court of Session declared that slavery was not permitted by Scots law.

**1778 The First Cotton Mill.** The mill at Rothesay

opened. The cotton industry developed rapidly: by 1780 a mill near Glasgow employed over 1,000 people, and by 1800 steam power was being used and the value of cotton production was three times that of linen.

**1782 The Highland Dress Proscription Act Repealed.** First passed after the Battle of Culloden as part of the disarming of the Highlands, the repeal confirmed that Jacobitism was seen as dead as a political force.

**1783 The *Glagow Advertiser* Launched** (later renamed *The Herald*). By 1800 more than twenty-five newspapers were being published in Scotland.

**1783 The Glasgow Chamber of Commerce Founded.** The first body of its kind in Britain, it was a sign of Glasgow's growing commercial and industrial importance.

**1786 Burns' Poems First Published.** Priced at three shillings and printed by John Wilson of Kilmarnock in an edition of just 612 copies, *Poems Chiefly in the Scottish Dialect* was an immediate success and made Robert Burns an overnight celebrity.

**1788 The World's First Steam-Powered Paddle Boat.** Designed by William Symington, the boat was launched on Dalswinton Loch, near Dumfries. Rabbie Burns was an early passenger.

**1788 The British Fisheries Society Founded**, to bring 'improvement' to the fishing industry, building new harbours throughout the Highlands.

## Adam Smith, 1723–90

The father of economics was born in Kirkcaldy and studied at Glasgow and Oxford universities. He thought little of Oxford, describing it as 'a sanctuary in which exploded systems and obsolete prejudices find shelter', and declaring that 'The greater part of [Oxford's] public professors have given up even the pretence of teaching.'

Back in Glasgow he was appointed to a professorship and lectured and wrote on philosophy. He also travelled on the Continent, meeting a number of celebrated intellectuals, and visited London, where he became a member of 'the Club', to which Dr Johnson also belonged. Smith was a well-known figure in Scottish Enlightenment circles and was particularly friendly with David Hume, whose obituary he wrote.

His *Wealth of Nations* was the first work to use 'economics' in its modern sense. Smith also coined the expression 'division of labour' and analysed the working of markets and currencies. He advocated the benefits of free trade, which he declared would promote international peace as well as increasing prosperity. He saw man as an economic animal and believed that a →

**1788 The Hanging of Deacon Brodie** for armed robbery. By day a respectable cabinet-maker and Edinburgh city councillor, by night Brodie was a burglar who used his ill-gotten gains to fund a gambling habit and support two mistresses. Robert Louis Stevenson, whose family knew Brodie, was inspired by the trial to write *The Strange Case of Dr Jekyll and Mr Hyde* (1886).

combination of self-interest and free competition meant the 'invisible hand' of the market could deliver prosperity for all. This linking of commerce and free trade with the idea of progress has been the world's dominant economic doctrine ever since Smith described it.

Smith never married (he was distinctly odd-looking, with bulging eyes and a big nose), lived with his mother and was a typically absent-minded professor.

He once had to be rescued from a tanning pit that he had walked into while discoursing on free trade; and he was observed putting bread and butter into his teapot, drinking it and then declaring it was the worst cup of tea he had ever tasted.

**1789 Inverary Castle Completed**, the home of the Dukes of Argyll and the first major neo-Gothic building in Britain.

**1791 Sir John Sinclair of Ulbster's *Statistical Account of Scotland* Published.** Sinclair was the first person to use the word 'statistics' in its modern sense, and his twenty-one-volume survey revealed among other things

# Robert Burns, 1759–96

Scotland's best-loved poet. Rabbie Burns was a poor tenant farmer's son from Alloway in Ayrshire. He was an avid reader who had absorbed an immense amount of literature by the time he began to work on the family farm and write his own verse.

Burns worked at a variety of jobs from farmer to exciseman, while conducting a string of affairs and fathering some fifteen children, six of them out of wedlock. He fell in love easily and often ('To see her is to love her') and his love affairs inspired some of his finest lyrics. He was also more than fond of a drink, declaring that 'Freedom and whisky gang thegither.' None of this endeared him to the Kirk or respectable society, but it gave him the raw material for poems that reflected the lives and loves of ordinary folk and his own belief that 'To step aside is human.'

His early political views were extremely radical:

> A fig for those by law protected,
> Liberty's a glorious feast
> Courts for cowards were erected,
> Churches built to please the priest.

→

In his thirties Burns became less radical, but his verses such as 'Scots Wha Hae' continued to express an intense patriotism and his views remained fundamentally democratic ('A man's a man for a' that').

Burns wrote verses in English, in broad Scots and in what might be called light Scots dialect. Many of his poems were adaptations of traditional folk songs and stories – perhaps the greatest being 'Tam O'Shanter', a long ballad of liquor, lust and witchcraft that he is said to have written in a single day. Despite his fame, when Burns died at the age of just thirty-seven he had not made much money from his pen, mainly because he wrote too little in the conventional high-flown style that publishers demanded. This refusal was precisely what made him Scotland's national poet, for his verse speaks to everyone.

Many of his lines have passed into proverbial use ('The best laid plans o' mice an' men gang aft a-gley'). Others express penetrating ideas in simple language ('O wad some Pow'r the giftie gie us, to see oursels as others see us'). His poetry presented the world with a Scottish national character that, far from dour Calvinism, delighted in everyday and sensual pleasures and was salted with pawky humour.

His poems have become part of the mental furniture of many Scots. Within five years of his death the first Burns club was established, and soon Burns suppers were being held on 25 January, the poet's birthday, with an address to the lassies, recital of his 'Address to a Haggis' and the singing of his song 'Auld Lang Syne'. The custom has spread throughout the world.

that nearly all Scots, at least in the Lowlands, could read and write.

**1791 John Howie's *Scots Worthies* Published**, a catalogue of the heroes and martyrs of the Reformation and Covenanting periods. The book's lengthy subscription list contained the names of many craftsmen and manual workers, confirming how far literacy had spread.

**1792 The Year of the Sheep.** Highland landowners had already started to 'clear' their estates of poor tenants to make way for more profitable sheep farming. This year saw a particularly high rate of clearances, as well as the first resistance to the landowners, by the men of Ardross in Ross-shire who combined to drive the sheep away.

**1794 The Execution of Robert Watt** for conspiring to kidnap the judges of the Court of Justiciary and seize Edinburgh Castle. In 1792 the Scottish Association of Friends of the People, inspired by the ideals of the French Revolution (1789), was formed by Thomas Muir to campaign for political reform, and riots and demonstrations were widespread in the 1790s. The authorities clamped down hard, especially Scotland's leading judge, the notorious Lord Braxfield. When a radical demonstrator he had sentenced to death protested that Jesus Christ himself had preached the brotherhood of man, Braxfield replied, 'Aye, and he waur hangit tae.'

**1797 Keiller's Marmalade First Sold**, made by Janet Keiller, wife of a Dundee merchant.

**1797 The Battle of Camperdown.** Admiral Adam Duncan, one of many Scots who made a career in the Royal Navy, defeated the Dutch navy .

**1797 Robert Stevenson Appointed Engineer to the Lighthouse Board.** In the next four decades he built eighteen lighthouses around the Scottish coast, and was the founder of a dynasty of 'Lighthouse Stevensons' – eight members of the family were involved in building almost a hundred more Scottish lighthouses in the next century and a half. The author Robert Louis Stevenson was his grandson.

**1800 The 'Colossus of Roads'.** Thomas Telford, began a twenty-year programme of improvements to road communications throughout Scotland. It became possible to travel from Edinburgh to London by stagecoach in less than three days.

**1800 The First Gaelic Bible Published.**

**1801 The Capture of *El Gamo*.** Thomas Cochrane in the sloop *Speedy* took the Spanish frigate *El Gamo*. This extraordinary victory – the Spanish ship was much larger – made Cochrane's name. The son of an impoverished aristocratic family from Lanarkshire, he went on to become an admiral, a radical politician and (as a freelance commander) a hero of the struggle by South American countries to free themselves from Spanish rule.

**1802 The *Edinburgh Review* Launched.** The magazine, which expressed liberal views, rapidly became very influential and was read all over Britain. It supported the Union,

## The Highland Clearances

In 1814 the families of the small townships of Strathnaver in the north of Sutherland were forcibly evicted from their homes. The houses were then burned by the order of Patrick Sellar, the factor (manager) for Elizabeth, Countess of Sutherland, the owner of Strathnaver and a million acres more. This was just one of many evictions on the Sutherland estates in the 1810s, and thousands of people were forced off the land that they and their ancestors had worked, to make way for sheep. The dispossessed were moved to coastal communities where they could not make a living except by working for their landlord, mainly by collecting kelp (seaweed), which was then used in various manufacturing processes. Sellar was put on trial for his actions, but of course was acquitted.

Between 1750 and 1860 many poor Highlanders were forced to leave their homes and emigrate or move south to the cities (by 1840 there were at least 25,000 Highlanders in Glasgow). Few of them had formal leases, and their landlords could evict them at will, often using violent methods in places where there were few witnesses. Some Highlanders still put a pathetic trust in the ancient bond between the chief and his *clann* (literally, children), but most chiefs had adopted expensive southern ways and many delegated the management of their estates to agents. There was a basic clash between the old attachment to their land of those who lived on it and the views of landowners, who were beginning to see their estates as commercial enterprises.

Emigration from the Highlands was not, of →

course, a new phenomenon, nor was it all the result of landlords clearing their tenants. Rapid population increase, combined with shortage of fertile land, meant that many Highlanders looked for opportunities abroad, especially after news filtered back from the earliest emigrants of the availability of land in America and Canada. Sometimes whole neighbourhoods took ship together across the Atlantic to found new communities in places such as Nova Scotia (*see* 1867).

There were different sorts of clearance at different times and in different places. The notorious Sutherland clearances were not aimed at getting rid of the people so much as 'improving' the landowner's estate. The people were simply seen a resource that could be better used as labour in the kelp industry than as tenants on land that could more profitably be turned over to sheep; and the landowners' misguided view was that wage labour was better for the moral welfare of the people than subsistence farming. When the kelp business collapsed, landowners started actively to encourage emigration, sometimes subsidizing it, sometimes simply evicting their tenants to fend for themselves as best they could.

The Clearances left a legacy of bitterness and hatred in the Highlands, only partly mitigated by the Crofting Acts (*see* 1886) and not forgotten today. There are still ruined houses in many glens, once flourishing townships but now part of often foreign-owned estates, where deer stalking and tourism have taken the place of the sheep whose wool, ironically, soon became unprofitable when faced with competition from Australian imports.

referring to Scotland as 'North Britain' and Scots as 'North Britons', and promoted 'improvement' in agriculture and commerce. The publisher was Archibald Constable, one of several famous names in this great age of Scottish publishing (others included Collins, Chambers, Blackie, Nelson, John Murray and Bartholomew).

**1803 The Caledonian Canal.** Work began on the canal linking the North Sea and Atlantic through the lochs of the Great Glen.

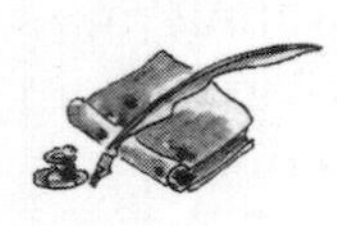

**1805 'The Lay of the Last Minstrel'**, a long and romantic narrative poem about an ancient feud in the Borders, brought instant fame to its author, Walter Scott.

**1805 Mungo Park Set Sail** on his second Niger expedition. Already an experienced explorer and the first European to reach the river Niger, Park, a prosperous farmer's son from Selkirk, declared he would 'discover the termination of the Niger or perish in the attempt'. True to his word, after a series of adventures and the death of nearly all his companions, Park was drowned in a battle with hostile natives.

**1806 The Last Impeachment of a Cabinet Minister.** Henry Dundas, Viscount Melville was impeached for misuse of navy funds. Appointed Lord Advocate in 1775, he managed politics in Scotland for Prime Minister William Pitt the Younger by handing out government patronage in return for political support. 'King Harry IX', as he became known, controlled virtually all of Scotland's parliamentary seats.

**1809 The Death of Sir John Moore.** The most notable

Scottish general of the Napoleonic Wars, Moore was fatally wounded at the Battle of Corunna. He was born in Glasgow, but like many upper class Scots he rarely visited his native land after his boyhood.

**1810 The World's First Savings Bank Founded** by Reverend Henry Duncan at Ruthwell in Dumfries to look after small sums saved by the poor.

**1812 Henry Raeburn Painted Alasdair Ranaldson MacDonald** of Glengarry in full Highland dress. Raeburn, also known for his celebrated picture of the skating minister, was, together with Allan Ramsay and David Wilkie, one of three great Scottish portraitists of this period.

**1815 The Battle of Waterloo.** Charles Ewart, a sergeant in the Royal Scots Greys, captured the regimental eagle of Napoleon's Imperial Guard. A giant of a man, reportedly of 'Herculean strength' and an expert swordsman, Ewart cut down three Frenchmen in seizing the eagle. When asked to tell his story at a banquet in 1816, he modestly said that he would rather refight the encounter than speak about it in public.

## Sir Walter Scott, 1771–1832

Walter Scott was born into a middle-class Edinburgh family and intended for a career in the law. But, like Rabbie Burns, whom he met soon after Burns achieved fame in 1786, Scott was fascinated by Scottish history and folklore. Even before 'The Lay of the Last Minstrel' made his name he had edited a collection of Border ballads, and after 1805 he devoted himself to writing. Other poems followed, including 'The Lady of the Lake', an Arthurian romance transplanted to Loch Katrine, and 'Marmion', an epic tale of the Battle of Flodden. In 1814, to raise money for his printing press, Scott wrote *Waverley*, the first of the novels that made him an international celebrity. It was set against the background of the Forty-Five, and later novels such as *Rob Roy*, *The Heart of Midlothian* and *The Bride of Lammermoor* continued to mine romantic episodes in Scotland's past.

→

In effect, Scott invented the historical novel and became in the process the bestselling writer of his day and the best-known novelist in the world. More than just a writer, he became a kind of unofficial guardian of Scottish history. He used the money from his enormous book sales to build Abbotsford House, near Melrose, an extraordinary building in the baronial revival style, and filled it with historical relics. In 1818 he secured royal permission to break into a locked room in Edinburgh Castle and found – amid a blaze of sensational publicity – the crown jewels of Scotland that had been lost since 1707. He was rewarded with a baronetcy, the first such honour ever conferred on a writer, and later stage-managed the elaborate pageantry of King George IV's visit to Edinburgh in 1822. Scott's last years were marred by the collapse of his publishing firm and the need to continue churning out books to keep his creditors at bay.

Scott's books have long been out of fashion and are now little read, but they were extraordinarily influential at the time. He virtually reinvented Scottish history, in particular rehabilitating the culture of the Highlands, which had been so tarnished by the Jacobite rebellions, and his books were a key influence in the Highland revival of the early nineteenth century. His critics say that he merely created a 'Scotland of the imagination', that he swamped Scotland's genuine history in 'tartanry' and promoted a falsely romantic image of the nation's past. Certainly it is true that his books gave a romantic and traditionalist slant to events, but he also grounded his stories in the everyday life of the country and the characters of ordinary men and women.

**1816 Robert Owen in New Lanark.** Owen set up an infant school at his New Lanark cotton mill, part of his advanced scheme of enlightened capitalism.

**1817 *The Scotsman* Launched**, initially as a weekly paper.

**1817 *Blackwood's Magazine* Launched.** Originally it was a Conservative rival to the Liberal *Edinburgh Review*.

**1820 The Battle of Bonnymuir.** A strike of 60,000 workers in the West of Scotland led to the appointment of a 'provisional government' in Glasgow, and some of the strikers marched on the Carron ironworks in an attempt to obtain weapons. The government called out the Stirlingshire yeomanry, and three protesters were killed in a skirmish at Bonnymuir, near Falkirk. Their leaders were subsequently sentenced to transportation.

# 1822
# GEORGE IV AND THE HIGHLAND REVIVAL

George IV, when he stepped ashore at Leith on 15 August, was the first British monarch to visit Scotland since 1651. He was already an enthusiast for the poetry of Ossian and the romances of Sir Walter Scott, and Sir Walter was determined to give the royal visitor a suitably historic welcome to his northern kingdom. Balls, parades and receptions were organized. Clan chiefs were summoned from the Highlands. The Kirk addressed the king, as did various loyal societies. Traditions were invented, such as converting the Royal Company of Archers into a king's bodyguard.

The prevailing tone of all these celebrations was not so much Scottish as Highland. Kilts, bonnets, tartans, bagpipe music and Gaelic battle songs were everywhere. The king himself – red-faced, enormously fat and panting after any exertion – appeared ludicrously dressed in a Royal Stewart kilt, feathered bonnet and flesh-coloured tights to hide his swollen legs, but was delighted with his enthusiastic reception as 'chief of chiefs' and with the romantic plaided panorama laid on for his benefit.

Of course, much of it was completely phoney. Not many real Highlanders actually turned up, and one of the few chiefs who did, Alasdair Ranaldson MacDonald of Glengarry, became a conspicuous nuisance by pushing himself forward at every opportunity. Lowlanders who would once not have been seen dead in a kilt scrambled to kit themselves out in tartan. Plenty of contemporaries saw how silly the whole affair was. One acutely observed, 'Sir Walter has made us appear to be a nation of Highlanders, and the bagpipe and the tartan are the order of the day.'

The Highland Revival – the fashion for traditional Highland culture – appeared just at the time when the genuine article was fading under the effects of emigration and the Clearances (the tiresome Glengarry was himself a notable clearer). Symbolic of this was the case of tartans and the kilt. Clan tartans were unknown until they were artificially created at this time – the traditional distinguishing mark of a clan was always its badge not its dress, and the traditional dress of Highlanders was not the kilt but the plaid, a length of woollen cloth that could serve as robe, cloak or bedding. The king's adoption of the short *philabeg* (little kilt), as worn by soldiers, meant that this now became

the accepted form of national dress, even for those Scots with no Highland connections. The primitive dress of those who had recently been seen as mountain bandits became the national costume of all Scots, as anyone attending a Scottish wedding or football international can see today.

★

**1823 John Loudon Macadam** invented the modern road surface by using tar to bind together the surface stones (known as 'macadamization' or 'tarmac').

**1823 Charles Macintosh,** the Glasgow chemist, patented a method for making waterproof garments (macintoshes) out of rubber.

**1823 James Hogg and *The Private Memoirs and Confessions of a Justified Sinner*.** It is a fantastic novel written in a mixture of English and broad Scots. If it can be said to have a single theme, it is the exploration of religious obsession. Hogg, known as the 'Ettrick Shepherd' was a poor farm worker who taught himself to read and write.

**1824 The Licensing of Whisky.** It has been estimated that the average Scottish male in 1800 drank about a pint of whisky (from the Gaelic *uisge beatha*, 'water of life') every week; and, as the century progressed, drams helped to dull the misery of life in the overcrowded slums of industrial towns. Heavy taxation on spirits was a great inducement to illegal distilling: despite the best efforts of the gaugers (excisemen), more than half of all the whisky drunk came from illegal stills, and the trade was winked at by many in authority, including the Kirk itself. The 1823 Licensing Act started to stamp out illegal distilling by encouraging operators to go legitimate – some of whisky's most famous names, such as Glenlivet, derive from what were once illegal stills.

**1826 The Douglas Fir.** The son of a stonemason from Scone, David Douglas led a botanical expedition to the Pacific North-West of America and returned with a wealth of new plants that transformed gardening and forestry, including the Douglas fir, one of which, at Stronardron in Argyll, is now Britain's tallest tree. In the twentieth century many Scottish hillsides were planted with Sitka spruce and Lodgepole pine, two of the other trees he discovered.

**1826 Scotland's First Railway Opened**, to carry coal from Monkland to Kirkintilloch on the Forth/Clyde Canal.

**1828 The Resurrection Men.** William Burke and William Hare, both immigrants from Ireland, murdered sixteen vulnerable men and women and sold their corpses to the Edinburgh Medical College for dissection by anatomists.

Hare got away free by giving evidence against Burke, who was hanged – and then dissected.

**1828 The Glasgow Cooperative Society Founded**, the first such organization to pay dividends to its members on the purchases they made.

**1829 Felix Mendelsson Visited Scotland.** He went to the island of Staffa, and subsequently wrote his *Fingal's Cave Overture*, inspired by the strange echoes within the cave.

**1831 The Glorious Twelfth.** The Game Act set 12 August as the start of the grouse-shooting season. As the century progressed, the 'Glorious Twelfth' became a key date in the social calendar of the upper classes, and grouse shooting, together with deer stalking and salmon fishing, drew increasing numbers of visitors to the Highlands from the south and from England, many of whom bought sporting estates.

**1832 The Scottish Reform Act.** The Act granted Scotland eight extra parliamentary seats at Westminster, expanded the electorate and standardized the voting qualifications. Reform was long overdue, since Scotland was full of rotten boroughs: the MP for Edinburgh was elected by just thirty-three voters and the county of Bute had only twelve voters, eight of whom were members of Lord Bute's family. The proportion of adult males qualified to vote jumped from fewer than one per cent to more than ten per cent, although very few working-class men were eligible. Only nine Tory MPs were returned for Scottish seats at the subsequent general election, and the Whigs (later Liberals) dominated Scottish politics until 1914.

**1834 Royal & Ancient.** King William III (IV of England) granted St Andrews Golf Club permission to call itself the 'Royal & Ancient'. The Open Championship was first played at St Andrews in 1873.

**1837 The Cotton Spinners' Strike.** The strike, which was against a reduction in wages, collapsed when the leaders were arrested and subjected to a show trial by the authorities, who were terrified of organized labour. Mechanization in the textile industry continued, and the trade unions became less militant.

**1837 Carlyle's *History of the French Revolution* Published**. Thomas Carlyle, the 'Sage of Ecclefechan', was one of Victorian Britain's most influential writers as a philosopher, essayist, satirist and historian. His life's work was an attempt to reconcile Christian values (although he lost his faith in formal religion) with the dramatic social changes caused by the Industrial Revolution and their interpretation by what he called the 'dismal science' of economics.

**1839 Chartism.** A National Chartist organization was established to mobilize working-class support for political reforms such as votes for all men and payment for MPs.

**1841 The Hungry Forties.** A sharp economic recession meant that a quarter of the population of Paisley were living on charity and the city's corporation went bankrupt.

**1841 Population Rise.** The Census revealed that Scotland's population had increased from 1.6 million to 2.6 million since 1801. The biggest increase was in the Central Belt, where the population more than doubled.

**1842 The Edinburgh and Glasgow Railway.** Railways spread rapidly, crossing the border in 1848, reaching Inverness in 1863, Wick in 1874, Stranraer in 1878 and Fort William in 1894.

# 1843
# THE DISRUPTION

On 18 May the established Church of Scotland split when more than a third of its ministers and about half its lay members walked out to form the Free Church. The crucial issue was lay patronage (the right of laymen, usually landlords, to 'intrude' candidates for the parish ministry), but Thomas Chalmers, the motivating spirit of the Disruption, had a broader agenda. He believed that urbanization and industrialization was leading to a breakdown of the traditional parish system, and that the Kirk was thus failing in its duty to the people. No longer content with attempts to revive the established Church, he now decided that the only option was to break away.

Within five years the Free Church raised £1 million from its supporters and had a national structure of 700 churches – often large conspicuous buildings designed to cock a snook at the established Church – as well as schools, a college and missions at home and abroad. Its radical nature, its rejection of landlord patronage and the fact that it spoke for the poor meant that great support was recruited, especially in the Highlands and the big cities.

The Disruption – the most traumatic of many such splits among Scotland's notoriously quarrelsome clergy – was a huge blow to the established Church of Scotland and greatly reduced its powers in areas such as poor relief and education as well as its claim to speak with authority on matters of personal and public morality.

★

**1846 Harris Tweed** first used as a trademark for cloth made by hand from wool dyed, carded and spun in the Outer Hebrides.

**1846 Cook's Tours.** Thomas Cook's 'Tartan Tours' were hugely successful, attracting customers from the USA as well as England and the Continent. A visit to Sir Walter Scott's house at Abbotsford was one of the tours' most popular attractions.

**1847 The Potato Famine.** By the end of 1846 and after two seasons of potato blight it was reckoned that three-quarters of the population of the North-West Highlands and the Outer Hebrides, all heavily dependent on the potato, had no food left. Private charity and some government aid saved the day, but at the cost of forcing people into work schemes that paid starvation wages for extremely hard labour.

**1848 The Queen at Balmoral.** Queen Victoria and Prince Albert leased the Balmoral Estate, which they later bought. The castle they built there was an extreme example of the Scots baronial style and heavily furnished in tartan. Lord Rosebery, a Scot and the queen's prime minister in the 1890s, called the drawing room 'the ugliest room in the world'. The queen became very attached to her Deeside home, publishing a sentimental account of *Our Life in the Highlands* (1868) and finding consolation for the death of

Albert in the company of John Brown, her Aberdeenshire ghillie and manservant.

**1848 New Zealand.** The Lay Association of the Church of Scotland founded Dunedin (the Gaelic name for Edinburgh) to be the main Scottish settlement in the colony of New Zealand. More than a fifth of all emigrants to New Zealand in the nineteenth century were Scots.

**1850 The World's First Oil Company.** James 'Paraffin' Young opened a plant at Bathgate to extract lubricating oils and paraffin from shale and coal.

**1850 *Monarch of the Glen* Painted by Landseer.** This iconic portrait of the defiant stag has adorned a million shortbread tins since, but was a less representative image of mid-nineteenth-century Scotland than Paraffin Young's grimy factory.

**1851 Urban Growth.** The Census showed that almost forty per cent of Scots lived in towns and cities. No other

European country apart from England was now so urban or had urbanized so rapidly. Glasgow was Scotland's largest city, with more than 330,000 inhabitants (it had trebled in size since 1801), and almost one in five Glaswegians had been born in Ireland. There was considerable prejudice against these Irish immigrants, seen as a degraded underclass who stole Scots' jobs and brought papist superstition with them. But a good many were Protestants from Ulster, who imported their aggressive form of Orange Protestantism and thus fostered sectarian strife

**1854 The Thin Red Line.** Britain under the leadership of an aristocratic Scottish prime minister, the Earl of Aberdeen, went to war against Russia in the Crimea. Sir Colin Campbell, who had risen through the ranks from his birth as a carpenter's son in Glasgow, commanded the Highland Brigade. At the Battle of Balaclava the 93rd Sutherland Highlanders were the only troops left to defend the base against a Russian cavalry attack. There were not enough of them to form squares, the usual defence against cavalry, so they formed a single line (the

'Thin Red Line') and broke the Russian charge with their disciplined musket fire.

**1857 The Indian Mutiny.** Crimean War hero Sir Colin Campbell was the man chosen to lead the army of 20,000 men sent to put down the mutiny, which he successfully did. Careful rather than dashing as a general, he was known to his men as 'Sir Crawling Camel'.

**1858 Alexander 'Greek' Thomson** completed the building of Holmwood, his most elaborate house, a Cathcart villa in the Greek Revival style from which he took his nickname.

**1859 Sanitation Came to Glasgow.** A supply of pure water from Loch Katrine was piped to the city. In 1862 a sanitary department was set up and in the following year a medical officer of health was appointed. All of this helped to prevent the recurrence of the cholera and typhus epidemics that had regularly ravaged Glasgow, but other cities were less fortunate. In 1861 Dundee had just five WCs for a population of 92,000.

**1859 Samuel Smiles' *Self Help* Published.** Smiles was the son of a small shopkeeper from Haddington, and his book was the bible of the classically Victorian and typically Scottish virtues of industry, thrift and self-improvement.

**1859 The National Gallery of Scotland** opened to the public. A fine neoclassical edifice, it was the last work of William Playfair, who was responsible for many of

Edinburgh's public buildings, including the Royal Scottish Academy and the Royal College of Surgeons' Hall.

**1860 James Clerk Maxwell** was appointed professor of natural philosophy at King's College, London. Born in Edinburgh and previously a professor at Aberdeen, Clerk Maxwell was still only in his twenties. His contribution to mathematics and theoretical physics, particularly in the field of electromagnetism, was the most significant of any nineteenth-century scientist. Einstein himself later declared that Clerk Maxwell's work was the most important since Newton.

**1861 Slum Life.** The Census showed that one-third of all Scottish households occupied a single room. Despite some improvements, the lives of most urban and many rural Scots were still lived in great squalor. The death rate remained high throughout the nineteenth century, and one in eight children died before their first birthday – the figures were far worse in the big cities. Not surprisingly, many Scots seized the opportunity to emigrate (two million of them between 1815 and 1914, proportionately more than three times the number who left England and Wales), and others sought relief in drink or evangelical religion.

**1862 *The Flying Scotsman.*** The express passenger train service between Edinburgh and London took ten and a half hours, including a thirty-minute lunch stop at York.

**1866 David Livingstone Set Out** to find the source of the Nile.

## David Livingstone, 1813–73

The most famous Victorian explorer of Africa and one of the great national heroes of the age was a typical 'lad o'pairts' who started work at the age of ten in a Lanarkshire cotton mill, while attending night classes to further his education. He first went to the 'dark continent' in 1840 as a missionary, and was saved from the jaws of a lion by an African comrade; but he was an unsuccessful evangelist, making, it is said, only one convert, and was increasingly drawn to exploration and his mission to end the slave trade, which was still engaged in by Arab and Portuguese traders.

His astonishing journey across Africa on foot in 1853–6 made his name. Starting from the Cape, he travelled north to modern Zambia, then to Luanda (Angola) on the Atlantic coast and then back to the east coast at Quelime (Mozambique). On the way he became the first European to see Victoria Falls, which he named after his queen, and formed the opinion that the Zambezi River was the key to opening up Central Africa. The journey made headlines across the world, and in 1858 the government sponsored Livingstone to return and explore the Zambezi. He spent a further six years doing so, but the river's rapids and cataracts proved unnavigable, and his wife died of malaria on Lake Malawi, which his expedition was the first to reach.

Undaunted, Livingstone set out from Zanzibar in 1866 to find the source of the Nile. Despite making further geographical discoveries, he failed to find the Nile's source, and after suffering innumerable hardships and constant illness, he lost contact with the outside world and was believed dead. In 1871 the *New York Herald* →

sent Henry Morton Stanley to find him, and this he succeeded in doing at Ujiji (in modern Tanzania), uttering the immortal words, 'Dr Livingstone, I presume.' Two years later Livingstone died, kneeling in prayer and racked with malaria and dysentery, near Lake Bangweulu (Zambia). His heart was buried in Africa, but two faithful servants carried his body 1,000 miles to the coast.

Livingstone was not an easy man to deal with: one of his companions on the Zambezi expedition declared 'Dr Livingstone is out of his mind and a most unsafe leader.' But his knowledge of medicine and preference for travelling light helped him to make friends easily with Africans and to cover remarkable distances. More than anyone else, he was responsible for opening up Africa to European colonization, and his belief was that 'Christianity, Commerce and Civilization' would deliver the continent from barbarism and slavery.

**1867 The First Canadian Prime Minister.** Sir John MacDonald, a native of Glasgow, became the first prime minister of the newly established dominion of Canada. In the two centuries following Wolfe's defeat of the French at Quebec about a million Scots emigrated to Canada, and some four million Canadians today claim Scottish ancestry. For many Scottish emigrants, drawn by the opportunity of land and jobs, Canada was almost an overseas Scotland, 'the country they could not have at home'. Many migrants were groups of Highlanders, and clan society was transported wholesale to parts of Canada, where Highland place names (Inverness, Glengarry, Banff) and Gaelic culture such as Highland games and traditional music still survive.

**1868 The Representation of the People Act.** The Act gave Scotland seven extra parliamentary seats at Westminster, but this was still an under-representation in proportion to population. Twelve more seats were granted in 1885, bringing parity with England closer.

**1869 Liptons Stores**. Thomas Lipton, a Glasgow shopkeeper's son, returned from America, where he had learned modern retailing methods. The chain of Liptons grocery stores he established, selling tea and food in small packages, was the ancestor of the modern supermarket.

**1871 The Calcutta Cup.** The Scots won the first rugby international against England by two tries (one converted) to one. Since 1878 the match has been played for the Calcutta Cup, so called because it was made from melted-down Indian silver rupees.

**1872 The Death of Greyfriars Bobby.** For fourteen years the faithful Bobby, a Skye terrier, guarded his master's grave in Greyfriars Kirkyard in Edinburgh. He is commemorated by a celebrated statue nearby.

**1873 The Scottish Football Association Founded.**

**1876 Alexander Graham Bell** (born in Edinburgh) took out the first patent for a telephone in the USA.

**1876 Mary Slessor** began her missionary work in Nigeria. The strong-minded daughter of a poor Aberdeen family, Slessor scandalized her contemporaries by living among poor villagers and adopting a number of Nigerian children. She gained the trust of the locals and set up churches, schools and hospitals, as well as promoting women's rights.

**1876 The First Chairs of Education** in Britain were established at Edinburgh and St Andrews Universities.

**1879 The Tay Bridge Disaster.** On 28 December the central section of the bridge collapsed as the Edinburgh mail train was crossing it, and the carriages plunged into the Tay. The disaster was the occasion for William McGonagall, the doyen of bad poets, to pen this deathless verse:

Beautiful railway Bridge of the Silv'ry Tay!
Alas! I am very sorry to say
That ninety lives have been taken away
On the last Sabbath day of 1879,
Which will be remember'd for a very long time.

**1879 Gladstone's Midlothian Campaign.** Totally Scottish by birth but completely English by upbringing, William Gladstone emerged from retirement to relaunch his political career by standing as parliamentary candidate for Midlothian. His series of speeches, some lasting for hours, was the first recognizably modern political campaign.

**1881 Up-Helly-Aa** began in Lerwick. This fire festival, still held on the last Tuesday in January, celebrates Shetland's Viking heritage.

**1882 The Battle of the Braes.** This was the name the newspapers gave to a clash between police and the crofters they were attempting to evict from their homes on Lord MacDonald's estate in Skye.

**1882 Clydebuilt.** More steamships were built on the Clyde than in the whole of the rest of the world and

'Clydebuilt' became the hallmark of quality craftsmanship married to high technology. Heavy engineering, especially those industries connected with shipbuilding, had become the cornerstone of the Scottish economy.

**1883 The Boys' Brigade** was founded in Glasgow, the world's first uniformed youth organization, which aimed to imbue boys with Christian values and to promote the British Empire.

**1883 The First Carnegie Library** was established in Dunfermline (*see* page 168).

**1884 Rothesay Pier Built.** The town was already an important holiday resort and a magnet, especially during Fairs Week in July, for working-class Glaswegians, who were now beginning to take holidays away from home.

**1885 The Scottish Office** was established as a government department and the position of Scottish secretary was revived.

**1886 The Crofters' Holdings Act.** This finally gave crofters in the Highland counties security of tenure, a guarantee of fair rent and the right of free sale of their crofts. However, the Act did not stop emigration depopulating the Highland counties.

**1886 John Boyd Dunlop**, an Ayrshire farmer's son, patented the pneumatic rubber tyre. Dunlop's development proved crucial to the bicycle and automobile industries.

**1886 The Scottish Labour Party** was founded, but made little electoral progress against the dominant Liberals.

## The Beautiful Game

Queen's Park, Scotland's oldest club and the only amateurs remaining in the Scottish League, took the lead in founding the Scottish Football Association (SFA), but within fifteen years the central rivalry of the 'Old Firm' clubs was in place: Rangers FC was founded in 1873, and in 1887 Celtic FC was founded by Brother Walfrid to provide healthy recreation for young Catholic men in Glasgow. In 1888, in the first Old Firm game Celtic beat Rangers 5–2 in a 'friendly' match; but their subsequent meetings have not always been so amicable, since the games became the focus of often violent sectarian rivalry between Protestant supporters of Rangers and Catholic supporters of Celtic, a conflict of prejudices that has not altogether disappeared even in the twenty-first century.

There was a centuries-old tradition of ba' games in many parts of the country – rough-and-tumble affairs with dozens of men and boys on each side, often including scrums and handling as well as kicking the ball. But once the rules of modern Association Football were established, attending football matches rapidly became the chief recreation of working-class Scottish males, and the game acquired an almost religious status among them. Many great Scottish players travelled south to seek their fortune, and there was a time when few of the big English clubs were without their dour Scottish defender or jinking inside forward.

Scottish clubs have won three European trophies (Celtic in 1967, Rangers in 1972 and Aberdeen in 1983), but Scotland's national team rarely performed well on the big stage. Victory over the old enemy at Wembley or Hampden Park was traditionally more highly →

**1886 William Mackinnon**, the Glasgow shipping magnate, founded the Imperial British East Africa Company.

**1891 Sir Hugh Munro's *Tables* Published**, listing the 283 peaks in Scotland over 3,000 feet, which have since become known as 'Munros'.

**1892 The First Gaelic Mod** was held in Oban, a festival of music and literature modelled on the Welsh Eisteddfod and designed to preserve and celebrate Gaelic language and culture.

esteemed than World Cup success, but Scotland's travelling supporters, the Tartan Army, acquired an international reputation for colourful good fellowship at a time when English fans were notorious for drunken violence.

Even at times when its game was in the doldrums, Scotland's footballing reputation was upheld by its managers. In 1986 Alex Ferguson was appointed manager of Manchester United. The most recent in a great line of tough football bosses from working-class backgrounds in the West of Scotland – Matt Busby, Bill Shankly, Jock Stein, among others – Sir Alex first made his name with Aberdeen and has led the world's most famous club to a string of successes.

# Andrew Carnegie, 1835–1919

In 1901 Andrew Carnegie sold his business and personally pocketed more than $350 million in the course of his life, making him the richest man in the world. But he was a most unusual plutocrat. He wrote, 'The amassing of wealth is one of the worst species of idolatry. No idol is more debasing than the worship of money.' True to this creed, he took a limited income from his business and gave away the rest – several hundred million – to a great variety of charitable causes.

Carnegie's life was a classic rags-to-riches story. He was born the son of a poor weaver in Dunfermline and emigrated as a boy with his family to the USA, as did almost a million other Scots in the century before 1914. Carnegie himself said, 'The United States would →

have been a poor show had it not been for the Scotch.' He started work in a cotton mill at the age of thirteen for $2 a week, progressing to jobs as a telegraphist and railway clerk. His early employers noted his extraordinary intelligence, hard work and perseverance, but his financial break came from shrewd investment of his hard-won savings in railroad companies, metal works and oil. This gave him the capital to start building up his own gigantic steel business.

As a boy, Carnegie had a passion for reading and educated himself widely. These intellectual interests persisted into adulthood, and he had many friends among writers, academics and politicians. He published several books, including *The Gospel of Wealth*, in which he proposed that the rich should use their money to help others, and *Triumphant Democracy*, which controversially criticized Britain's monarchy and praised the democratic constitution of the USA.

Carnegie did not forget his native land. He bought Skibo Castle in Sutherland, where he spent part of each year, and his first Carnegie Libraries – there were eventually 3,000 all over the world – were in Scotland. He was a devotee of Burns, in particular an admirer of his democratic ideals, and he instructed that all his libraries should contain Burns' *Complete Works* and exhibit a bust of the poet. Among the causes he supported were spelling reform, world peace and education for African-Americans and he also gave money to universities, scientific institutions and churches.

## Scots and the Empire

'[I] have found myself in many distant lands. I have never been in one without finding a Scotchman, and I have never found a Scotchman who was not at the head of the poll.' These words of the imperialist Prime Minister Benjamin Disraeli were certainly true of the management of the British Empire by Scots in the nineteenth and twentieth centuries. Henry Dundas (*see* 1806) controlled the East India Company, which ran British India, and he promoted many Scots within it. Lord Dalhousie governed India in 1848–56 and did more to change the country than any governor before him. Lachlan Macquarie governed New South Wales from 1810 and oversaw its transformation from a harshly disciplined penal colony to a society of free settlers. From 1850 to 1939 almost a third of all colonial governors were Scots.

Disproportionate numbers of missionaries (*see* 1876) and explorers (*see* 1805, 1826, 1866) came from Scotland. Scottish regiments were to the fore in all the wars →

**1892 Keir Hardie Elected to Parliament** for the London constituency of West Ham.

**1893 The First Women Graduated** from Scottish universities. No women were permitted to graduate from Oxford or Cambridge until the 1920s.

**1893 The 'Wee Wee Frees'**, the Free Presbyterians, split from the Free Church.

of empire, and about a third of the officers in the Indian army were Scots. The colonies of settlement (Australia, New Zealand, Canada, South Africa) attracted great numbers of Scottish immigrants, as did the commercial opportunities of empire: the Hudson's Bay Company was dominated by Scots, especially Orkneymen; the opium trade between India and China was exploited by the partnership of Jardine and Matheson, formed in 1827; and the trading activities of Mackinnon's East Africa Company resulted in formal British colonization of Kenya, Zanzibar, Tanganyika and Uganda.

In the heyday of the British Empire the Union with England was hailed as the 'Imperial partnership' and Glasgow boasted of being 'the second city of Empire'. Scotland's schools and universities produced a surplus of well-qualified professionals – teachers, engineers, lawyers, scientists – and the empire provided employment for this growing middle class. Emigration to the empire was seen as evidence of the adventurousness and virility of the nation, and thus the powerful image of the 'Enterprising Scot' was born.

**1895 The *Daily Record*,** the first halfpenny paper, was launched in Glasgow.

**1896 The Scottish Trade Union Congress (STUC) Founded.** It was a more radical body than its English equivalent, set up almost thirty years earlier.

**1897 Glasgow School of Art**, the masterpiece of architect Charles Rennie Mackintosh, was completed in two phases.

## James Keir Hardie, 1856–1915

In 1892 the House of Commons, an assembly of gentlemen in top hats and tailcoats, was startled by the appearance of a new member in a tweed suit, red tie and deerstalker. This was James Keir Hardie, recently elected as the first Labour MP. He proceeded to astonish Parliament further by advocating high taxation of the rich, women's suffrage, old age pensions, free schooling and independence for British India, as well as proposing to abolish the House of Lords. When the Commons voted to congratulate the royal family on the birth of a prince in 1894, he declared he would only vote with the House if the message included an expression of condolence to the families of the 251 coalminers recently killed in an explosion in Wales.

Hardie was born the illegitimate son of a serving maid (Keir was his mother's name, Hardie his stepfather's) and grew up in grinding poverty in Lanarkshire. He went out to work at the age of eight, became a coalminer at eleven and was frequently the main breadwinner in his family. He never attended school, but his mother taught him to read and write. In 1880 he led a miners' strike and was dismissed, after which he worked as a journalist and in 1886 became secretary of the Scottish Miners' Federation. In 1888 he stood for Parliament in the mining constituency of Mid-Lanark as the first ever independent Labour candidate, but lost heavily to the Liberal.

In 1893 he was instrumental in founding the Independent Labour Party (ILP) and in 1900 was a member of the Labour Representation Committee (LRC), which developed into today's Labour Party. Although he served as chairman of the party, he was not a good party →

man. His political ideas were shaped by his strong religious faith, and he held to them dogmatically. His firm belief in votes for women and his committed pacifism at the outbreak of war in 1914 led to disputes with many of his colleagues.

In 2008 a poll at the Labour Party Conference rated him 'Labour's greatest hero'.

The exterior of the building showed an extraordinary mix of influences – medieval castle, Japanese design, the arts and crafts movement, art nouveau and modernism – yet they worked together to produce a harmonious whole; the airy, wood-panelled interior was just as beautiful.

**1900 Harry Lauder** made his first London music hall appearance, the start of a career that made him the best-paid entertainer in the world and a friend of royalty and the rich. Lauder's songs ('I Love a Lassie', 'Roamin' in the Gloamin'' and many others), his tours of the USA and his charity work made him the best-known Scotsman in the world. Winston Churchill called him 'Scotland's greatest ever ambassador', but he has also been criticized for presenting a comic Scottish stereotype – alcoholic, tight-fisted, kilted and sentimental – which has never entirely disappeared.

**1900 The Wee Frees** split from the Free Church and attracted strong support in Gaelic-speaking areas.

**1901 Population 4.5 Million.** The Census showed Scotland's population was now almost 4.5 million, as against 1.6 million in 1800, and two-thirds of Scots (compared to little more than a third in 1800) lived in the Central Belt. More than half the population lived in towns and cities, as opposed to just a third fifty years earlier, and one in three Scots lived in the four big cities, Edinburgh, Glasgow, Aberdeen and Dundee. Seventy per cent of households in Glasgow still occupied one- or two-room dwellings, and the high-rise tenement buildings characteristic of Scottish cities meant that they were more overcrowded than their English counterparts.

**1901 Irn Bru**, Scotland's 'other national drink', was first produced by AG Barr of Cumbernauld. Until 1946 it was known as 'Strachan's Brew', but then a change in the law meant a change of name, since the drink is not technically 'brewed'. Irn Bru's ingredients are secret and its effect as a hangover cure is legendary.

**1903 Major-General Sir Hector Macdonald Committed Suicide**, after accusations (later proved groundless) of homosexuality. A crofter's son from Easter Ross, 'Fighting

Mac' rose through the ranks, saw service in a number of colonial wars and became a popular hero. He was allegedly the model for the Scottish officer depicted with a Sikh soldier on the label of Camp Coffee jars.

**1905 Scots Rule Westminster.** The Liberal leader Henry Campbell-Bannerman, son of the Lord Provost of Glagow, succeeded Conservative Arthur Balfour, member of an East Lothian landowning family, as prime minister. Balfour was later succeeded as Conservative leader by Andrew Bonar Law, born in Canada of Scots descent and employed in the family ironwork business in Glasgow. Between 1905 and 1911 three of the four chairmen of the parliamentary Labour Party (Keir Hardie, Arthur Henderson and Ramsay MacDonald) were Scottish.

**1906 D.C. Thomson Started in Dundee**. The company published newspapers, magazines and books but became most famous for their comics and comic strips, including

'Oor Wullie', 'The Broons', *The Dandy* and *The Beano*, which first appeared in the 1930s. The success of the firm put the third 'J' in Dundee's traditional 'three Js' (jam, jute and journalism).

**1913 Herring Fishing Reached its Peak.** There were so many fishing boats in Wick that it was said that you could walk dry-shod right across the harbour. Tens of thousands of Scots, many of them women, followed the fleet down the east coast to England as seasonal workers. Skilled fisher girls could gut a herring in a second, and their cure for salt-blistered fingers was to apply porridge.

# 1914–1918
## THE FIRST WORLD WAR

In 1914 patriotic war-fever resulted in a flood of volunteers, even greater in Scotland (where nearly twenty-seven per cent of males eventually joined the armed forces) than in England and Wales (just over twenty-four per cent). Men from many workplaces, clubs and neighbourhoods formed 'pals battalions', and the height restrictions were waived so that the 'wee hard men' who had grown up short of stature in Scotland's deprived areas could enlist too. Poverty and chronic unemployment meant that men in some places jumped at the chance – Dundee, for example, had the highest proportion of servicemen of any British city.

When the British Expeditionary Force left for France in 1914, 22 of its 157 battalions were Scottish, and even the Lowland regiments wore the kilt, as they had done since the 1880s. 'Jocks', as Scottish soldiers were (and are) known, took part in all the great actions on the Western Front – Loos (1915) was the battle with the highest proportion of Scottish units, three full divisions – and they acquired a reputation for bravery and dash, as well as the respect of the Germans, who christened their kilted enemies the 'ladies from hell'. From 1915 to the end of the war the commander-in-chief of the British army was a Scot, Field Marshal Douglas Haig, a member of the well-known Edinburgh whisky family. Of the half million Scots who fought, almost 100,000 were killed, and in some areas such as the inner cities and the Outer Hebrides the proportion of deaths was even higher.

Scots at home also found their lives changed. Many women went out to work as 'clippies' on the buses and trams, or in munitions factories. The Clyde basin was the most important centre for armaments production in Britain, and the war gave a great stimulus to Scottish heavy industry. Full employment and trade union militancy led to a wave of strikes in 1915–16 over issues such as 'dilution' (women taking men's jobs, at lower pay), housing shortages, rent increases and war profiteering by employers. The strikes foreshadowed what became known as 'Red Clydeside' (*see* 1919) and the move by working men and women to support Labour instead of the Liberals, who increasingly appeared to be the bosses' party. The five-man war cabinet that ran the war effort from 1916 contained two Scots, Arthur Henderson (Labour) and Andrew Bonar Law (Conservative).

★

**1915** ***The Thirty-Nine Steps***, the most famous novel by John Buchan, a minister's son from Fife, was published. Buchan was also a lawyer, journalist, historian, civil servant and politician, and in 1935 he was made Baron Tweedsmuir and became Governor General of Canada.

**1918 The Representation of the People Act.** This gave the vote to all men over twenty-one, and to women over thirty. The Scottish electorate jumped from 779,000 to over two million.

**1919 The German High Seas Fleet Scuttled in Scapa Flow.** Fifty-two warships were deliberately sunk on 21 June by order of Admiral von Reuter to avoid their falling into British hands. No British ships were present, and the main witnesses to the greatest loss of shipping ever experienced on a single day were a party of Orcadian schoolchildren.

# 1919

## RED CLYDESIDE

On 31 January some 100,000 people gathered in George Square, Glasgow, at a rally organized by trades unions to support striking workers and to protest at high rents, poor housing, unemployment and low pay. Although the intention of the demonstrators was peaceful, the response of the authorities turned the occasion into a riot. Witnessing the red flag being brandished, they believed that this was the start of a planned socialist revolution – the Scottish secretary, Robert Munro, called it a 'Bolshevist rising'; they ordered the Riot Act to be read and sent in a police baton charge to break up the crowd. The demonstrators,

including many war veterans, fought back, and widespread brawls ensued. The government then sent in troops, not the conveniently placed Scottish units at Maryhill Barracks, who were locked in for fear they might join the demonstrators (as had happened during the recent Russian Revolution), but English troops accompanied by tanks.

This was the most dramatic episode in what came to be called 'Red Clydeside', the era of political radicalism in the Glasgow area from the 1910s to the early 1930s that took the form of trade union activism, anti-war protest and campaigns for social reform.

In fact, the Red Clydesiders' militancy has been exaggerated by legend. They were not genuine revolutionaries, as was the hope of some of their supporters and of those on the left who still speak of January 1919 as Scotland's 'lost revolution'. Certainly, the leadership of Red Clydeside included some charismatic individuals – John Maclean, who was appointed Soviet consul in Scotland, called the First World War 'this murder business' and was arrested six times between 1916 and 1923; and James Maxton, of whose wildly bohemian appearance it was said, 'He didn't just preach the revolution, he looked it.' But a communist revolution in Scotland was never a realistic proposition. The strikes of 1919 collapsed, some of the organizers of the George Square demonstration were jailed, and although several of the Red Clydesiders were elected to Parliament in 1922, they were thus forced to work for change through the democratic process.

★

**1921 Unemployment Touched Twenty Per Cent.** Post-war recession hit Scotland especially hard, since the economy had been artificially stimulated by wartime demand for heavy industry, which now came to a halt. Wage rates in Scotland began to slip behind those of the rest of the UK.

**1922 A Labour Breakthrough.** The party won thirty-two per cent of the Scottish vote and twenty-nine seats.

**1924 *Chariots of Fire*.** Eric Liddell, known as 'the flying Scotsman', broke the world record for the 400 metres at the Paris Olympics after refusing to run in the 100 metres because the event was held on a Sunday – a story made famous by the 1981 film *Chariots of Fire*. Liddell, who was also a rugby international, later became a missionary in China, where he died in a Japanese prison camp in 1945.

**1924 The First Labour Government was Elected** with Ramsay MacDonald as prime minister.

**1925 The Birth of Televison.** John Logie Baird, an engineer and inventor from Helensburgh, gave the first public demonstration of images transmitted by television.

**1926 Hugh McDiarmid and 'A Drunk Man Looks at the Thistle'.** This long poem was a meditation on the condition of Scotland and reflected McDiarmid's nationalist, Anglophobic, atheist and communist beliefs. He was a leading figure in the so-called Scottish Renaissance of the inter-war years: a group of writers, including Neil Gunn (*Highland River*), the poet Edwin Muir and Lewis Grassic Gibbon (*A Scots Quair*), who shared nationalist and left-wing beliefs as well as a dislike of the 'kailyard' school of folksy, escapist fiction. Far better known to the general public were the popular novelists of the period such as A.J. Cronin, Compton Mackenzie, John Buchan and Eric Linklater.

**1926 The General Strike Collapsed** in Scotland as in England. McDiarmid's disappointed response was recorded in the lines, 'The thistle like a rocket soared/ an' cam' doon like the stick.'

**1927 John Reith was Appointed Director-General** of the newly formed BBC. A serious-minded son of the manse, Reith saw radio and television as tools of education not entertainment.

**1928 Alexander Fleming Discovered Penicillin** *(see* page 186).

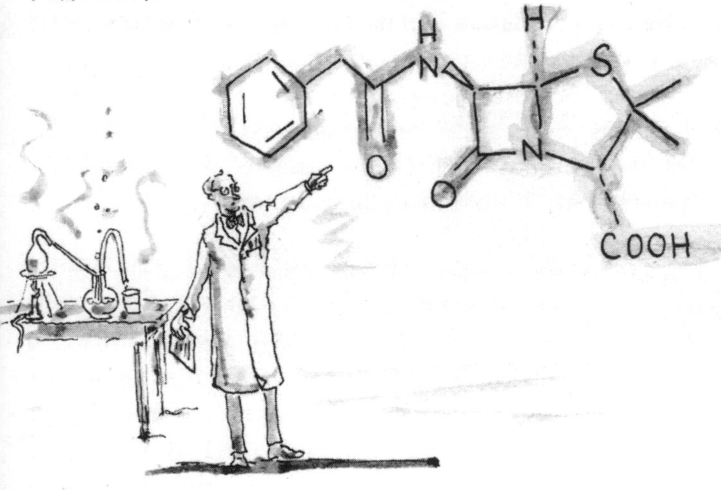


**1930 The Evacuation of St Kilda.** The last thirty-six inhabitants of Scotland's most remote islands were resettled at their own request in Argyll. St Kilda is now a UNESCO World Heritage Site.

# James Ramsay MacDonald, 1866–1937

MacDonald's career was perfect embodiment of the dictum, 'all political careers end in failure.' In 1924 he reached the top of the political tree as the first Labour prime minister; but just over a decade later and prime minister once again, he resigned in poor health, stumbling and incoherent in public, allied to a Conservative Party that distrusted him and loathed by his former Labour comrades.

James Ramsay MacDonald was born in Lossiemouth, the son of an unmarried housemaid called Mary Ramsay (MacDonald was his father's name). He moved to London at the age of twenty, where he worked as a clerk, attended science classes and became involved in Labour politics. In 1897 he married Margaret Gladstone, who shared his socialist views but whose family money financed his political career and allowed the couple to travel frequently abroad. He was elected Labour MP for Leicester in 1906 and became Labour leader for a second time in 1922.

His government of 1924 had time to pass an Act providing decent and affordable accommodation for council tenants, but was forced to resign after less than a year as a result of the faked Zinoviev letter, which suggested that Britain was heading for communism. In fact, MacDonald was keen to present Labour as a party of moderation: he did not support the General Strike of 1926 and appeared on formal occasions in the conventional top hat and tail coat. Neither action endeared him to his socialist colleagues. →

In 1929 he returned to power as prime minister of another minority Labour government, but this one was scuppered by the Wall Street Crash and the worldwide economic depression that followed. In 1931 MacDonald became prime minister of a National Government in coalition with Conservatives and Liberals, but Labour performed disastrously in the general election and MacDonald was reviled as a traitor by most of his own party.

MacDonald was in many ways a born leader, heroically handsome, with great presence and a thrilling, musical voice. But his talents were also his undoing: his great oratory could seem to be woolly rhetoric, he was just a little too conscious of his good looks, and after his wife died he became snobbishly susceptible to the charms of society hostesses such as Lady Londonderry.

## Alexander Fleming, 1881–1955

Fleming was a farmer's son from Ayrshire who left school at sixteen to work in a shipping office, but then took advantage of an inheritance to study medicine. On 28 September 1928, and by now a bacteriologist at St Mary's Hospital, Paddington, he returned from holiday to find some culture dishes in his laboratory contaminated by fungus. He was notoriously careless about his equipment and thought little more of it – but then he noticed that no bacteria were growing in a zone around the fungus. He isolated the active agent in this mould and christened it 'penicillin'.

Fleming published his results in 1929; they attracted little attention. He continued to work on penicillin for a decade but found it difficult to produce in quantity, and his clinical tests proved inconclusive. It was the work of three others, Ernst Chain, Howard Florey and Norman Heatley, that led to the development, trialling and mass production of the antibiotic.

Penicillin proved to be the most valuable of all antibacterial agents and saved hundreds of millions of lives. Fleming, who had originally been inspired to work in bacteriology by witnessing wounded men dying from septicaemia in the First World War, was modest about his accidental discovery. 'I certainly didn't plan to revolutionize medicine,' he later said, but that was just what he did. He was awarded the Nobel Prize for Medicine in 1945.

**1931 The Invergordon Mutiny.** Sailors of the Atlantic fleet at its base in the Cromarty Firth refused to obey orders for two days as a protest against proposed pay cuts. The mutiny caused panic in the stock market and a run on the pound, and was a major cause of Britain coming off the gold standard, just a few days later.

**1932 Unemployment Topped Twenty-Seven Per Cent**, and remained at over twenty per cent for most of the 1930s. This figure masked even worse conditions in some places such as Airdrie and Motherwell, where more than one in three people were out of work. Scotland suffered more than England because of its dependence on heavy industry and because it lacked the south's new, electric-powered, consumer-oriented industries such as car making. The wealth gap began to widen, although the north of England shared some of Scotland's economic woes. A typical publication of the period was G.M. Thomson's *Scotland: That Distressed Area.* Unemployment, coupled with poverty and bad housing, resulted in the poor health of many Scots, whose height, weight, diet and life expectancy suffered in comparison to the rest of the UK. The 1931 Census showed that the population was shrinking (a total of 1.7 million Scots emigrated between 1911 and 1991).

**1933 Nessie Spotted.** The *Inverness Courier* published stories and letters about the existence of a 'monster' in Loch Ness. This marked the beginning of worldwide interest in the mysterious creature.

**1934 The Scottish National Party (SNP)** was formed, as a result of a merger between the left-wing National Party of Scotland and the right-wing Scottish Party. From the start the new party found it difficult to agree where it stood on the political spectrum. The party had no answer to Scotland's pressing economic and social problems and made no impression at the polls.

**1934 Valvona & Crolla Founded in Edinburgh.** The famous delicatessen originally served Edinburgh's Italian community. Italians immigrants started arriving in large numbers in the late nineteenth century, and Scotland now has, by some estimates, 100,000 people of Italian descent. Many made their living in the catering trade and opened ice-cream shops and cafes, even in small country towns.

**1935 Willie Gallacher Elected** as the Communist MP for the mining constituency of West Fife. A former Red Clydesider, Gallacher remained an MP until 1950 and a communist to the end of his life in 1965, by which time he had become an icon for Scottish socialists.

**1937 The Big Match.** A crowd of 149,547 people – a British and European record that will probably never be broken – attended a football match against England at Hampden Park in Glasgow. Scotland won 3–1.

**1938 The Iona Community Founded** by George MacLeod to train and support ministers who worked in inner-city and industrial parishes. Initially criticized by some as being 'halfway to Rome and halfway to Moscow', the community is now internationally known and respected.

**1938 The Empire Exhibition in Glasgow.** Despite a very wet summer, twelve million visitors attended the exhibition, which did much to revive the economy of the west of Scotland and restore morale after the dark days of the Depression.

**1938 The *Queen Elizabeth***, the largest passenger ship in the world at the time, was launched at John Brown's yard on the Clyde.

# 1939–1945

## THE SECOND WORLD WAR

As in 1914–18, Scotland shared the wartime experiences of the rest of Britain, and the war perhaps even enhanced a sense of 'Britishness' in the face of the common enemy. More than 30,000 Scottish servicemen were killed in action and some 5,000 civilians died in air raids. Evacuation of the cities took place in 1939, but in general Scotland suffered less than England from bombing by the Luftwaffe – the only really severe episode being the Clydebank blitz of 13–15 March 1941, in which two 200-bomber raids left more than 1,000 people dead and scarcely a house undamaged.

Scotland's geographical position had vital strategic implications: the 'Shetland Bus' was a sea-borne operation to support the Norwegian resistance movement, and convoys with war materials for Russia sailed to Archangel and Murmansk from Scottish ports. Most importantly of all, Scotland provided the shortest transatlantic route. In June 1942 the first contingent of 10,000 US troops disembarked in the Clyde from the *Queen Mary*, and many thousands of Americans and Canadians followed them in the months building up to D-Day. Prestwick became the world's busiest airport as American bombers started to arrive in huge numbers.

Scotland's economy was revived by the wartime demand for heavy industry. The revival had started in the late 1930s as

Britain started to re-arm, and by 1943 five ships a week were being launched on the Clyde. Tom Johnston, a charismatic former Red Clydesider and the Labour secretary of state for Scotland in the wartime coalition government, did much to mobilize the war effort in Scotland. Churchill, fearing nationalist sentiment in Scotland, gave Johnston a very free hand and he introduced central planning in a number of areas. Johnston set up the Scottish Council on Industry to maintain good industrial relations, the North of Scotland Hydro-Electricity Board to exploit the natural resources of the Highlands, the Scottish Tourist Board with a view to Scotland's post-war economy and, most remarkably of all, a scheme in the west of Scotland that was a forerunner of the National Health Service.

★

**1940 The 51st Highland Division Taken Prisoner.** On 12 June two brigades of the 51st (Highland) Division, about 10,000 men, surrendered to overwhelming German forces at St Valéry. They had been ordered to stay put in order to cover the retreat of the rest of the British Expeditionary Force and to stiffen the morale of the French, and

they continued to fight on after the evacuation from Dunkirk. The Highlanders spent the rest of the war in German prison camps where three of their officers invented the rousing dance, the Reel of the 51st.

**1941 Whisky Galore.** The SS *Politician*, sailing across the Atlantic with a cargo including 28,000 cases of whisky, was wrecked on 5 February on the island of Eriskay in the Outer Hebrides. Boats came from far and wide to salvage the bounty (whisky was in short supply under wartime regulations), but a spoilsport customs officer had a number of men charged with theft and, to the disgust of the locals, had the ship and her cargo blown up – though not before thousands of bottles had 'disappeared'. The incident became the basis of a novel by Compton Mackenzie and a celebrated Ealing comedy shot on location in Barra in 1949.

**1941 Rudolf Hess Landed in Scotland.** In one of the strangest episodes of the war, Hitler's deputy Hess flew solo across the North Sea and parachuted out of his Messerschmitt over Eaglesham in Renfrewshire on 10 May. He claimed he had come to offer peace terms to Britain (in advance of the German attack on Russia that took place weeks later), and the man he wished to offer them to was the Duke of Hamilton, who he believed to be an opponent of Churchill. Hess was promptly arrested, later tried at Nuremberg and sentenced to life imprisonment, which he served at Spandau Prison in Berlin, the last twenty years as its sole prisoner. Hess' flight and his long imprisonment thereafter have been fertile ground for conspiracy theorists.

**1945 The First SNP MP.** Robert McIntyre was elected in a by-election at Motherwell.

**1947 The Edinburgh Festival.** Launched as the 'Edinburgh International Festival', it originally offered music, theatre, opera and dance. In its first year it was gatecrashed by a number of independent theatre companies, and their contribution has since grown into the enormous Festival Fringe. The month-long festival now also encompasses film, literature, comedy and the visual arts, and is the biggest such event in the world.

**1948 The Tattoo** was first performed at Edinburgh Castle.

**1950 Stealing the Stone of Destiny.** On Christmas Day four students from Glasgow University broke into Westminster Abbey and removed the Stone of Scone. In the process they accidentally broke the stone in two – although it has two iron handles it was not easy to move, weighing more than 150 kg – but they managed to smuggle both pieces back to Scotland. Having made their point and after having the stone professionally repaired, they left it, wrapped in a saltire, in the ruins of Arbroath Abbey, from where it was taken back to London.

**1951 Below the Poverty Line.** The Census showed that a quarter of Scots still lived in one- or two-room dwellings; one-third of households shared a toilet.

**1953 Elizabeth II Crowned**, but the coronation provoked protests in Scotland, since she was only Elizabeth I of Scots.

**1954 Return of the Ospreys.** The birds were exterminated in 1916 by gamekeepers and egg collectors, and their

return to breed at Loch Garten in Inverness-shire was a great boost to the tourist trade in the Highlands.

**1954 Sorley MacLean**, the greatest Gaelic writer of modern times, published 'Hallaig', his poem about the desolation left by the Highland Clearances.

**1955 Conservative Scotland.** In the general election the Conservatives won thirty-six seats and an absolute majority of votes in Scotland. It was, in fact, a 'small-c conservative' period: the nation's two favourite TV programmes were *The White Heather Club* – wholesome kilted fun – and *Dr Finlay's Casebook,* nostalgic small-town drama.

**1956 Cumbernauld New Town Founded.** New towns were planned settlements containing residential, commercial and industrial areas, and designed to accommodate people moving out of the slum areas of the cities. The others were East Kilbride (1947), Glenrothes (1948), Livingston

(1962) and Irvine (1966). The new towns certainly offered pleasanter living conditions than the overcrowded and decaying inner cities, but many of their inhabitants felt they were dull and lacked a sense of community.

**1959 Nuclear Power.** The fast-breeder nuclear reactor at Dounreay in Caithness came on line, and within three years was providing power to the national grid. The potentially dangerous site was chosen deliberately to be as far as possible from London and south-east England.

**1960 Holy Loch** in the Firth of Clyde became a base for US nuclear submarines. Three years later, Faslane, not far away, became the base for the UK's nuclear submarines, now armed with Trident missiles.

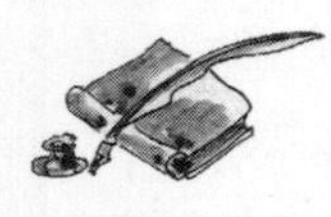

**1961 Muriel Spark's *The Prime of Miss Jean Brodie* Published**, a classic Edinburgh novel.

**1961 Dr Hastings Banda**, formerly an elder of the Kirk, became prime minister of the newly independent Malawi.

**1962 Sean Connery** made his first appearance as James Bond in *Dr No.*

**1963 Lord Home Became Prime Minister**, succeeding Harold Macmillan. Both men were Old Etonians and Scots of a sort – Home a landowner from Berwickshire and Macmillan the great-grandson of an Arran crofter – but otherwise very different. Macmillan was a cunning operator who presided over great growth in economic prosperity and the dismantling of the British Empire; his successor was a more straightforward character, who admitted using

# Sean Connery, 1930–

The best-known Scotsman in the world and the definitive screen Bond, Connery was born into a working-class family in Edinburgh. His first job was as a milkman, and he also served in the navy and worked as a labourer and lorry driver. His route into acting was through appearances as an artist's model and a body builder. Ian Fleming, the author of the Bond books, called Connery 'an over-grown stunt man' when he was chosen for the part, but was soon won over by the actor's physical presence and his charismatic performance in *Dr No*.

In six more Bond films and a string of other hits Connery went on to become one of the biggest international stars, but was notorious for playing every role in his gruff Edinburgh accent. He announced his retirement from acting several years ago.

He is a supporter of the SNP, to whom he has given substantial sums and much publicity at home and abroad. He more recently proclaimed his support for a referendum on Scottish independence. His critics point to the fact that he does not live or pay taxes in his homeland.

matchsticks to work out economic problems and soon lost power to Labour's Harold Wilson, who mocked Home's 'grouse-moor' image.

**1965 The Highlands and Islands Development Board (HIDB) founded**, to promote and coordinate economic and social development in the area.

**1967 A Great Year for Scottish Football.** In April Scotland beat 1966 World Cup winners England 3–2 at Wembley. In May Celtic won the European Cup by beating Inter Milan 2–1 in Lisbon. Every single one of Celtic's team, the 'Lisbon Lions', was born within a thirty-mile radius of Glasgow.

**1967 The *Queen Elizabeth II* (*QE2*) Launched** on the Clyde, the last great liner to be built there.

**1967 The SNP's Electoral Breakthrough.** Winnie Ewing won the by-election at Hamilton, overturning a Labour majority of 16,000 and giving notice that the SNP was now a force to be reckoned with in Scottish politics.

**1969 Catherine McConnachie Became the First Woman Minister** in the Church of Scotland, more than twenty years before the Church of England accepted women as priests.

**1970 Nationalist Disappointment.** The SNP won just one seat in the general election. The political fortunes of the nationalists in the 1970s seemed to reflect a protest vote against London government (as in Margot MacDonald's stunning by-election win at Govan in 1973) rather than a genuine desire for independence or even devolution.

**1971 The Upper Clyde Shipbuilders Work-In.** Once Scotland's industrial lynchpin, shipbuilding on the Clyde now employed just 8,000 men. When Upper Clyde Shipbuilders went into receivership the government refused a loan to keep the group going. The workforce, led by a young communist shop steward, Jimmy Reid, started an unauthorized 'work-in' to complete existing orders and show that the company was still viable. They received huge public support, and the government was forced to step in and support the yards, which remain in business today.

**1975 North Sea Oil.** The first oil was piped ashore at Peterhead. Aberdeen became a boom town on the back of the oil industry, which also brought money and jobs to Shetland and much of the north-east and the Highlands.

Nationalists saw what was produced in the North Sea as 'Scotland's oil'.

**1975 Billy Connolly Appeared on TV** on the *Parkinson* chat show. He told jokes that were considered near the knuckle at the time ('Did you hear about the man who buried his wife upside down so he'd have somewhere to park his bike?'), but the show was the breakthrough for Connolly's startlingly rude brand of comedy, in which bodily functions, personal confessions and his former life as a Glasgow boilermaker all played a part.

**1976 The Bay City Rollers Reached No 1** in the American charts. For a brief period of 'Rollermania' the clean-cut boys from Edinburgh in their tartan-trimmed outfits were the biggest band in the world.

**1977 The West Lothian Question.** Tam Dalyell MP asked the question: why should Scottish MPs at Westminster be

able to vote on purely English matters when English MPs would not be able to vote on matters such as education and health that would be devolved to a future Scottish Parliament? The question, prompted by the fact that the SNP had eleven MPs at Westminster, has still not been satisfactorily answered.

**1978 The Barnett Formula Devised**, to work out the proportion of government spending allocated to the different parts of the UK. Scotland receives more per capita than England, but this is justified by factors such as low density of population in much of the country.

**1978 Runrig Released Their First Album.** They were the first band to blend rock successfully with Scottish folk music, singing some songs in Gaelic and playing bagpipes alongside electric guitars.

**1979 The First Devolution Referendum.** In order to retain support in the face of challenges from the SNP, the Labour government agreed to hold a referendum in Scotland on whether to establish a devolved Scottish

Assembly. On a turnout of almost sixty-four per cent on 1 March there was a narrow majority in favour, but the government had set a condition that at least forty per cent of the electorate should vote 'yes', so the move failed. Under headlines announcing 'A Nation Divided' the newspapers declared that 'A third wanted it, a third didn't, and a third didn't care.'

Three weeks later, the SNP MPs' votes were crucial in passing the vote of no-confidence that led to Prime Minister Callaghan resigning and losing the subsequent general election to Margaret Thatcher's Conservatives. Devolution was now definitely off the political menu.

**1980 Olympic Gold.** Alan Wells won the 100 metres at the Moscow Olympics. He dedicated his victory to the memory of Eric Liddell (*see* 1924).

**1981 Alasdair Gray's *Lanark* Published.** This long book, written over the course of thirty years, was an extraordinary mix of fantasy, realism and postmodernism, set in Glasgow, sometimes depicted by Gray as the city of 'Unthank'. It has been declared one of the landmarks of twentieth-century fiction, although its author tended to debunk the praise of critics and offered instead the advice, 'work as if you live in the early days of a better nation.'

**1983 *Local Hero*,** Bill Forsyth's hugely successful film, was released. It was a wacky comedy with folksy overtones and did much to popularize the image of Scotland abroad.

**1983 The First Episode of *Taggart* Shown.** It is now the world's longest-running TV police series, set in Glasgow.

**1984 Grand Slam.** Scotland's rugby team won the Grand Slam for the first time since the 1920s.

**1985 The Gartcosh Steel Works Closed.** Under the Thatcher government's ruthlessly monetarist and free market economic policies unemployment reached nearly sixteen per cent. Although the Scottish economy did start to move away from its old dependence on heavy industry towards services, electronics, light engineering and tourism, Thatcher became very unpopular with most Scots, who saw her as a classic 'little Englander'.

**1987 DI Rebus Created.** Ian Rankin published the first of his 'Inspector Rebus' novels, set in Edinburgh.

**1988 Piper Alpha Disaster.** In the world's worst-ever offshore oil disaster 167 men died and just 59 were saved from a burning rig in the North Sea.

**1988 Lockerbie Crash.** A Boeing 747 (Pan Am Flight 103) was destroyed by a terrorist bomb. All 259 passengers were killed, as were eleven people in Lockerbie, where the plane fell. Two Libyans were subsequently convicted of planting a bomb in the plane's luggage compartment.

**1988 *Rab C. Nesbitt* Aired.** BBC Scotland first broadcast Ian Pattison's series featuring Rab, the string-vested 'street philosopher' from Govan, played by Gregor Fisher, who stumbled through more than fifty episodes of the blackly comic and very rude sitcom. English viewers needed subtitles.

**1989 Poll Tax.** Mrs Thatcher's government introduced the poll tax to replace local rates. Its introduction in

Scotland a year ahead of England was seen as discriminatory and the tax itself as deeply unfair. In some areas a third of people refused to pay, and the episode confirmed the unpopularity of Thatcher and the Conservative Party with most Scots.

**1989 Lord Mackay of Clashfern**, the Lord Chancellor and an elder of the Free Presbyterian Church (the 'Wee Wee Frees'), was suspended by his Church for attending the funeral of a Roman Catholic friend. This display of religious bigotry led to a split in his Church and thus the formation of a body that might ludicrously be called the 'Wee Wee Wee Frees'.

**1990 Glasgow – European City of Culture.** This was the culmination of the 'Glasgow's miles better' campaign, aimed at shaking off the city's old image of social deprivation and violence. Another key moment in this largely successful initiative was the opening of a magnificent new museum to house the Burrell Collection.

**1993 Irvine Welsh's *Trainspotting*** was published. Set among Edinburgh's drug-using underclass, the novel rapidly achieved cult status and presented its readers with a distinctly uncosy picture of Scotland's capital and favourite tourist destination.

**1994 James Kelman's *How Late It Was, How Late* Won the Booker Prize**. This tale of an ex-convict was set in Glasgow and written in broad dialect with liberal use of swear words. An English critic called the Booker award 'a disgrace'.

**1994 John Smith**, the leader of the Labour Party, often seen as Labour's 'lost prime minister', died and was buried on Iona.

**1995 *Braveheart* Released**, starring Mel Gibson as William Wallace. The film was full of glaring historical inaccuracies but it aroused huge interest in Scotland and swelled support for a revived Scottish Parliament.

**1996 The Stone of Scone Was Returned to Scotland** by John Major's Conservative government, exactly 700 years after King Edward I stole it, in a vain attempt by Major to stave off demands for devolution and to recover support in Scotland.

**1996 Dolly the Sheep Born,** the first animal ever to be cloned from an adult cell, an operation performed at the Roslin Institute, Edinburgh.

**1996 'Silicon Glen'.** This was the name given to the area around Livingston, where over 50,000 people were employed by firms making more than a third of Europe's personal computers.

**1997 New Labour and Devolution.** A general election

brought New Labour to power promising a referendum on devolution. In this election the Conservatives won not a single parliamentary seat in Scotland. The referendum delivered a 75/25 majority in favour of a Scottish Parliament and also approved that it should have tax-varying powers.

# 1999
# THE SCOTTISH PARLIAMENT REOPENS

'The Scottish Parliament, adjourned on the 25th day of March 1707, is hereby re-convened.' With these words, Winnie Ewing, presiding as its oldest member, brought Parliament back to life. Elected by a more proportional system than Westminster, about a third of the MSPs were women and six parties were represented – the Greens and the Scottish Socialists each picked up a seat. The Executive was a coalition of Labour, the biggest party, and the Liberals. Donald Dewar, the former Labour secretary of state and the man who shepherded the devolution legislation through the House of Commons, was elected first minister.

The Parliament had a rocky start. Donald Dewar died in 2000, and his Labour successors were not men of the same

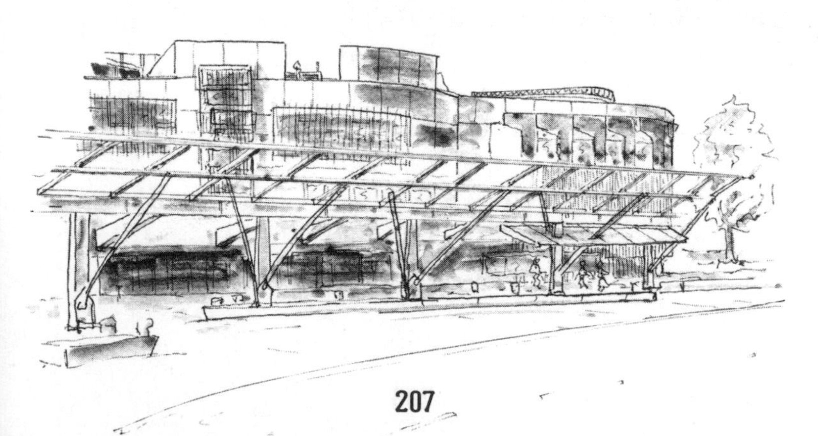

stature. There was an unseemly row over the abolition of Clause 28 (against the promotion of homosexuality in schools), and the Executive appeared toothless when it was unable to stop Mike Tyson, a convicted rapist, from flying into Glasgow. Worst of all, there was the escalating cost of the new Parliament building, originally budgeted at £50 million but coming in, when it was finally opened in 2004, at a cool £414 million. Not all observers liked the exterior of Enrico Miralles' building, but many who went inside were then won over by the quirky, asymmetrical, organic appearance of the interior.

In its first decade, Parliament had a mixed reception from the Scottish people. It was occasionally derided as a talking shop and its members seen as second class when compared to MPs at Westminster. But it passed some groundbreaking legislation. Smoking was barred in public places ahead of a similar ban in England. The introduction of free care for elderly people reflected Scotland's strong communitarian spirit, and the abolition of university tuition fees its traditional commitment to education. Parliament became a symbol of Scotland's national identity, which in the last few decades has emerged strong and distinctive, despite 300 years of political union with England.

**2007 Victory for the SNP.** The nationalists emerged as the biggest party from the third general election to the Scottish Parliament. They formed a minority government, with SNP leader Alex Salmond as first minister.

**2007 Gordon Brown**, a son of the manse from Kirkcaldy, became prime minister.

## Donald Dewar, 1937–2000

Often called 'the father of the nation', a title he modestly disclaimed, Dewar was more than anyone responsible for devolution and the revival of the Scottish Parliament. A Labour MP since 1966, he had pushed for devolution long before it became party policy, and after being appointed Scottish secretary by Tony Blair in 1997 he worked tirelessly to create the Scotland Act. When he took his seat at the opening of Parliament he was greeted with spontaneous applause from all round the chamber.

A skilled parliamentarian, a brilliantly witty speaker and an expert behind-the-scenes fixer, First Minister Dewar dealt competently with the early difficulties of the coalition Executive. But that did not explain the extraordinary scenes of mourning, unprecedented for a Scottish politician, when he died suddenly of a brain haemorrhage. He was mourned so deeply because he was loved and respected, not just by those who dealt with him professionally but by ordinary members of the public.

Tall, gangly and notoriously unkempt, Dewar was the very opposite of the manufactured politician. What you saw was what you got. He resisted all attempts to smarten up his appearance and despised the arts of the spin-doctor. Although a cultured and well-read man, he was just as happy discussing football with his constituents, and could often be seen in the streets of Glasgow, getting his own shopping.

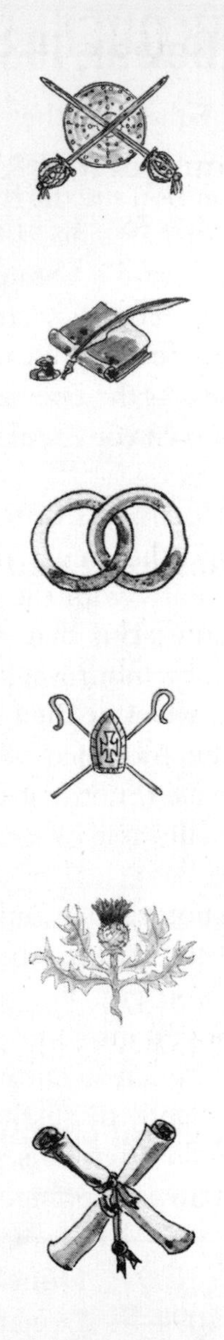

# KINGS AND QUEENS OF SCOTS

## House of MacAlpin

| | |
|---|---|
| 843–58 | Kenneth I |
| 858–62 | Donald I |
| 862–76 | Constantine I |
| 876–8 | Aed |
| 878–89 | Eochaid and Giric |
| 889–900 | Donald II |
| 900–43 | Constantine II |

## House of Dunkeld

| | |
|---|---|
| 943–54 | Malcolm I |
| 954–62 | Indulf |
| 962–6 | Duff |
| 966–71 | Culen |
| 971–95 | Kenneth II |
| 995–7 | Constantine III |
| 997–1005 | Kenneth III |
| 1005–34 | Malcolm II |
| 1034–40 | Duncan I |
| 1040–57 | Macbeth |
| 1057–8 | Lulach |

## House of Canmore

| | |
|---|---|
| 1058–93 | Malcolm III (Canmore) |
| 1093–4 | Donald III (Bane) |
| 1094 | Duncan II |
| 1094–7 | Donald III (restored) |
| 1097–1107 | Edgar |

| | |
|---|---|
| 1107–24 | Alexander I |
| 1124–53 | David I |
| 1153–65 | Malcolm IV (the Maiden) |
| 1165–1214 | William I (the Lion) |
| 1214–49 | Alexander II |
| 1249–86 | Alexander III |
| 1286–90 | Margaret (the Maid of Norway) |
| 1290–2 | Interregnum (the Great Cause) |
| 1292–6 | John Balliol |
| 1296–1306 | Interregnum (English rule) |

**House of Bruce**

| | |
|---|---|
| 1306–29 | Robert I (the Bruce) |
| 1329–71 | David II |

**House of Stewart**

| | |
|---|---|
| 1371–90 | Robert II |
| 1390–1406 | Robert III |
| 1406–37 | James I |
| 1437–60 | James II |
| 1460–88 | James III |
| 1488–1513 | James IV |
| 1513–42 | James V |
| 1542–67 | Mary (Queen of Scots) |
| 1567–1625 | James VI (and I of England 1603–25) |
| 1625–49 | Charles I |
| 1649–60 | Interregnum (the Commonwealth) |

| | |
|---|---|
| 1660–85 | Charles II |
| 1685–9 | James VII (and II of England) |

## House of Orange

| | |
|---|---|
| 1689–94 | William and Mary |
| 1694–1702 | William II (and III of England) |

## House of Stuart

| | |
|---|---|
| 1702–14 | Anne |

After 1707 Scotland and England were united. The subsequent kings and queens of England were automatically kings and queens of Scots.

# INDEX

## Principal Events, Topics, Names and Places


Aberdeen 57, 61, 62, 130, 163, 166–7, 174, 199
Adam, Robert 125
Agricola 5, 7–8
agriculture and fisheries 103, 116, 150, 176
Anglo-Scottish relations (*see also* Border, Forty-Five, 'Rough Wooing', Wars of Independence) 21, 24, 25, 27–9, 31, 35, 56, 63, 65–6, 67, 69, 70, 71, 81, 109–10, 111–13, 115, 127–8, 151
Arbroath, Declaration of 45–6
Auld Alliance 36, 52–3, 65, 72, 75

Baird, John Logie 182
Balliol, King John 36–8
Balmoral 155
Bannockburn, Battle of 3, 43–4
Berwick 38, 49, 60
Berwick, Treaties of
  (1357) 50
  (1560) 76
  (1586) 81
Bishops' Wars 92
Bonny Prince Charlie 2, 120–5
Border (Anglo-Scottish) 22, 28, 29, 33, 48, 51, 56, 60, 153
Borders region 11, 32, 41, 60, 61, 63, 67, 83–4, 85–6, 132, 142
Boswell, James 128–9
Bothwell, Earl of 78
*Braveheart* 2, 41, 205
Brodie, Deacon 134
Brunanburh, Battle of 21
Buchan, John 179
Burns, Robert ('Rabbie') 112, 133, 136–7, 144, 169

Caledonian Canal 142
Calgacus 7
Cameronians 102
Camerons 102, 120
Campbells 105–6, 117, 157, 158
Carlyle, Thomas 152
Carnegie, Andrew 165, 168–9
Charles I 89, 90, 91–2, 93–4, 95
Charles II 95, 96–7, 99–100, 102, 103
Civil Wars 79, 92–4, 96–7
Claim of Right 104
Cochrane, Thomas 139
Columba 12–13, 20
Commonwealth 98–9
Constantine II 21
Covenant, National 91–2, 96, 100, 103–4
Covenanters 91–2, 93–5, 96, 100, 101
  'Killing Time' 102–4
Cromwell, Oliver 94, 95, 96, 99

Culloden, Battle of 2, 122–3, 124
Cumberland, ('Butcher') Duke of 122–3

Darien Scheme 108–9
Darnley, Lord 77–8, 79
David I 27–9
devolution 201–2, 205–8
Dewar, Donald 207, 209
Douglas family 47, 49, 55, 58, 59, 60, 66
Douglas, Gavin 64
Dunbar, Battle of 96
Dunbar, William 63–4
Dundee 138, 158, 174, 175–6, 177
Dunlop, John Boyd 165
Duns Scotus, John 40–1

economy 49–50, 116, 125, 133, 140–1, 143, 181–2, 183, 186–7, 191, 195, 198
Edinburgh 22, 126, 130, 131
  *Edinburgh Review* 139
  Festival 193
education 60–1, 76, 86, 87, 101, 106, 117, 131, 146, 154–5, 160, 163, 183, 208
Edward I, 'Hammer of the Scots' 38–42, 46
Elizabeth I 75, 77, 78, 79, 82–3, 85
Enlightenment 117, 130–1

Falkirk, Battles of
  (1298) 39
  (1746) 122
famine 44, 89, 106, 155
Fleming, Alexander 183, 186–7
Flodden, Battle of 65–6
'Flower of Scotland' 44
'Flowers of the Forest' 66
football 163, 166–7, 188, 198
Forty-Five, The 120–3
Free Churches 154, 170, 174, 204

Gaelic 16, 20, 24, 33–4, 54, 61, 113, 129, 139, 147–8, 149, 156, 162, 167, 195, 201
George IV 147–9
Glasgow 32, 126, 130, 157, 158, 171, 199, 204
  Red Clydeside 180–1
  School of Art 171
Glencoe massacre 105–6
golf 59, 68, 119, 152
Graham of Claverhouse (Bonny Dundee) 101, 104
Greyfriars Bobby 163

Hadrian's Wall 8–9, 10
Halidon Hill, Battle of 49
Hamilton, Patrick 67
Hardie, James Keir 170, 172–3
Hebrides 5, 11, 12–13, 25–6, 33, 34, 57, 80, 86, 110, 132, 183
Henryson, Robert 62
Highland clearances 138, 140–1, 165, 195
Highlands 54, 86, 93, 101, 105–6, 119, 123, 126, 140–1, 157, 162, 165, 191

dress 133
'Revival' 147–9
Hume, David 117, 118–19, 130

industry 125, 126–7, 129, 132–3, 138, 139, 142, 146, 150, 152, 153, 155, 163, 164–5, 178, 189, 198
Inverness 12, 77, 122, 153, 162, 187
Iona 12–13, 188, 205

Jacobites 2, 3, 104, 105, 109, 112, 113, 114, 115–16, 120–5, 133, 144–5
James IV 61, 63
James VI and I 63, 78, 80, 83, 85–6, 87, 88

Killiecrankie, Battle of 104
Kirk 76, 80–1, 88, 92, 99, 100
prayer book riots 90
the Disruption 154–5
Knox, John 72, 73–4, 75

Lauder, Harry 173
law 16, 27, 33, 68, 94, 101, 103, 130–1, 132
Livingstone, David 3, 159, 160–1
Loch Ness Monster 13, 187
Lockerbie disaster 203
Lords of the Isles 34

Macadam, John Loudon 149
Macalpin, Kenneth 20
Macbeth 22, 23, 67
MacDonald, James Ramsay 184–5
MacDonalds 61–2, 80, 105–6, 124, 125, 148, 162, 164, 174
McGonagall, William 163–4
Macintosh, Charles Rennie 149
MacLeods 61–2, 80
Maid of Norway 1, 34–5
Malcolm III, Canmore 22, 24, 25, 46
Margaret, Saint 24
Marston Moor, Battle of 93
Mary, Queen of Scots 59, 69, 70, 71, 72, 77–8, 79, 82–3
Mons Graupius, Battle of 7
Montrose, Marquis of 93–4, 96
Morton, Earl of 80
Munros 89, 167, 180

Napier, John 88
Naseby, Battle of 94
Nechtansmere, Battle of 15–16
North Sea oil 199–200
Northumbria 14, 15, 22

'Old Pretender', *see* James Stuart
Orkney 5, 23, 33, 35, 60, 171, 179
Ossian 129–31, 147
Otterburn, Battle of 55

Park, Mungo 142
Picts 9, 10, 11, 12, 15, 19, 20
Piper Alpha disaster 203
Pope 31, 32, 45, 48, 51, 75–6

population 126, 135–6, 153, 156–7, 159, 174, 194
Prestonpans, Battle of 120

Raeburn, Henry 143
Red Clydeside 180–1
Reformation 75–6
religion (*see also* Civil Wars, Covenant, Covenanters, Free Churches, Kirk, Pope) 10, 12–13, 14, 17, 20, 25, 60, 67, 71, 72, 73–4, 107, 113, 117
Rizzio, David 77–8
Rob Roy 114–15, 116
Robert the Bruce 1, 2, 13, 41–2, 43–4, 46–7
Romans 5–11
Rosslyn Chapel 58
'Rough Wooing' 70, 71, 72
rugby 162, 203

*Sassenach* 16
Scot, Michael 32
*Scotsman, The* 146
Scott, Sir Walter 1, 115, 142, 144–5
Scottish National Party (SNP) 187–8, 193, 197, 199, 201–2, 208
Scottish parliaments 3, 33, 98, 104, 111–13, 200–1, 202, 205–6, 207
Shetland 33, 60, 164, 190, 199
Smith, Adam 130, 132, 134
Solway Moss, Battle of 69
Standard, Battle of the 28
Stevenson, Robert Louis 134, 139
Stirling Bridge, Battle of 39
Stone of Destiny (*aka* Stone of Scone) 33, 38, 193, 205
Stuart, James, 'Old Pretender' 109, 113, 116
Synod of Whitby 14

Tay Bridge disaster 163
Telford, Thomas 139
Tippermuir, Battle of 93
trade and commerce 27, 51, 54, 62, 71, 86, 106, 108, 117, 126, 133, 151, 162, 167, 188

Union, Act of 2, 111–13, 115
union of the crowns 85–6
universities 57, 61, 117, 163, 170

Vikings 18, 20

Wallace, William 2, 38–41, 46, 205
Wars of Independence 2, 38–50
Waterloo, Battle of 143
Watt, James 129
Whiggamore Raid 94–5
whisky 149
(SS *Politician*) 192
William the Lion 30–1
Wishart, George 71, 73
Wolf of Badenoch 54, 55